Thomas Merton
and the
Education of the Whole Person

Thomas Merton
and the Education
of the Whole Person

Thomas Del Prete

Religious Education Press
Birmingham, Alabama

Lbrary of Congress Cataloging-in-Publication Data

Del Prete, Thomas,
   Thomas Merton and the education of the whole person/Thomas Del Prete.
   Includes bibliographical references.
   ISBN 0-89135-074-8
   1. Merton, Thomas, 1915-1968—Contributions in Catholic theology of education. 2. Education (Christian theology)—History of doctrines—20th century. 3. Catholic Church—Education-History—20th century.
I. Title.
BT738.17.D44   1990   89-27775
261.5—dc20   CIP

Religious Education Press, Inc.
5316 Meadow Brook Road
Birmingham, Alabama 35242
10 9 8 7 6 5 4 3 2

Religious Education Press publishes books exclusively in religious education and in areas closely related to religious education. It is committed to enhancing and professionalizing religious education through the publication of serious, significant, and scholarly works.

PUBLISHER TO THE PROFESSION

Contents

Preface

Though it is not often recognized or acknowledged, I believe we all have a spiritual hunger. So it was that, when introduced to the work of Thomas Merton, like many before and after me, I was immediately drawn in. Merton became, and remains, an important source of inspiration and guidance for me on what he called the "real journey of life," the "interior" journey.

Up to the point when I was introduced to Merton's work, I had been involved in educational endeavors of various sorts; soon after, I was immersed in the study of education at graduate school. In spite of the broadened perspective I began to gain there from exposure to impressive social scientific, psychological, and philosophical schools of thought, I felt vaguely dissatisfied. While certainly illuminating in many respects, these perspectives rarely invited me to consider the nature of education by asking first of all what it means to be a whole person and to live, breathe, and grow on this earth. They sometimes caused me but never directly asked me to think about the nature of education by considering first of all that the person *is* and not, rather, what or how the person may do or think. None, certainly, asked me to think about education in relation to the "interior" journey, to the spiritual life.

It is no doubt indicative more of the general nature of modern Western education than any lack in my graduate program of studies that the topics which emerged as most compelling to me were addressed least. Be this as it may, my continued reading of Merton and my understanding of some of his basic concerns and questioning, together with a kind of irrepressible interest that seemed always to accompany me, convinced me that they ought to be. I naturally turned to Merton for help and decided that he would be the lens through which I would focus questions, ideas, and central themes. This book is the result of that effort. Essentially, I have tried to regard education in the Christian spiritual perspective provided by both Merton's life and work. This has meant exploring Merton's basic idea that "[education] means the formation of the whole person."

This book does not provide a methodology or a program; it would be very disappointing if approached as a "how to" book. It is concerned more with basic perspectives and understandings. It may, inasmuch as Merton so often does, call into question or help reformulate basic assumptions and accordingly alter one's sense of purpose or approach in education; or it might elicit insights from or provide perspective for the reader concerned about "the formation of the whole person" and about the nature of education in Western society and his or her actual role in it from a Christian spiritual point of view.

It is difficult to read from or about Merton's work without encountering Merton himself and, finally, oneself. To the extent that this is one's experience, it reflects, I would say, the challenging and deeply personalistic nature of Merton's example and message, regardless of context. To the extent that it is one's experience as a result of reading this work, it can be viewed similarly as an indication of the kind of educational experience that I believe Merton would highly value. The starting and ending points of a study of Merton and education are ultimately the same—ourselves; whatever insight we might gain vis-à-vis the purpose of education will be gained in proportion to our openness to understanding and deepening our understanding of our own selves as whole persons.

Along the journey from deep interest and vague notion to more coherent understanding which characterized the evolution of this work, I have appreciated the support, direct or indirect, of Robert Coles, Eleanor Duckworth, Richard Katz, Sara Lawrence Lightfoot, Henri Nouwen, Donald Oliver, and Parker Palmer. Fr. John Eudes Bamberger and Fr. Jean Leclercq provided encouragement during the first tentative steps. Robert Coles, Donald Oliver, and Parker Palmer were thoughtful readers of this work during its various stages. Their words resonated faith and assurance at different important times; their own work has been helpful and inspiring. Robert Daggy, Director of the Thomas Merton Studies Center at Bellarmine College in Louisville, Kentucky, was an invaluable aide in the research effort. Brother Patrick Hart was ever-gracious and fraternal in his unstinting support. This final printed version benefited greatly from the scrutiny and care of Barbara Scarbeau—my special thanks to her. I am especially grateful for the warm support of my colleague, Meg Kirkendall, for the good-humored support of my friends, and for the patient and loving support of my family. They were all in some sense allies in this effort, for in their own unique and special ways they helped me to understand better what and why I was trying to write. To Karen, my wife, I extend my warmest and deepest gratitude; she was so often by my side during this journey, always ready to help, always sustaining with her encouragement and willingness to listen, always present with her love.

1

Introduction

Thomas Merton (1915-1968) lived most of his adult life as a monk and contemplative in the Trappist monastic community called Gethsemani, in Kentucky. As "Thomas Merton" (he was known as "Father Louis" or "Louie" within his religious community) he had a public persona, established with the publication of his celebrated autobiography, *The Seven Storey Mountain*, in 1948.[1] Merton became well-known through this moving account of the intellectual and spiritual odyssey that brought him to Gethsemani. In subsequent years his work expanded along with his reputation. He became recognized widely as an exceptional spiritual writer, poet, and social commentator, and for his efforts on behalf of peace, ecumenism, East-West religious dialogue, and social justice.

Merton's written legacy includes an extraordinary collection of over fifty-five books and two hundred fifty essays, many short prose pieces, a weighty volume of poems, and letters, reflecting a large and diverse group of correspondents, numbering in the thousands. This body of literature stands in large part as a record of Merton's understandings and experiences gathered on what he called the "real journey of life"—the "interior" journey.[2] For Merton, this journey consisted primarily in the effort to know God as fully as possible and to live by love. This constituted the essence of his vocation as a "contemplative" and the purpose of his monastic life.[3] Merton had no illusions, on a personal level, as to the difficulties entailed by this journey; as a contemplative he was, in his own words, an "explorer . . . [of] a desert area of [the human] heart."[4] Yet neither could he

5

be more convinced of the extreme importance of a sense of the interior and spiritual life not only for himself but for everyone for whom the assumptions of life reflected in secular Western society in the twentieth century had become acceptable wisdom. Thus Merton's cumulative written narrative is both a remarkable account of his own interior journey in the twentieth century and the record of a journey intentionally shared. For in sharing from the depths of his personal experience as a contemplative Merton was clearly hoping to awaken others to the spiritual dimension of their own lives.

Like Henry David Thoreau before him, who recorded in *Walden* the results of his "experiment" in learning "to live deliberately," Merton provided the world with a chronicle of his learning as a contemplative explorer of the heart.[5] Also like Thoreau, Merton brought his insights critically and constructively to bear on the public conscience of his society. Distinctively, Merton's attention was not directed so much at the effort "to live deliberately" as to the spiritual imperative to find and to live according to his true identity on the deepest possible level. Whereas Thoreau cast his work in the design of an experiment, Merton cast his in the form of a spiritual search with the most profound implications for the integrity and quality of his life. This personal search eventually led him to consider more fully his relationship to his fellow human beings.

Merton's fundamental social concern was for the modern, particularly Western, world's loss of a sense of interiority and therefore its disconnection from a true sense of reality and spiritual identity; as he expressed it in the period just before his death, "It is the peculiar office of the monk in the modern world to keep alive the contemplative experience and to keep the way open for modern technological man to recover the integrity of his own inner depths."[6] It was a central aim of his teaching efforts, both in his monastic community and through writing that reached the secular world, to enable others to recover their inner identity and restore that connection. He firmly believed that the people of his world would thereby become more whole, more human, more free, and more capable of loving.

Along the path of his own interior journey, then, Merton strove to communicate to others something of their essential reality as persons. Similarly, focusing through the finely ground lens of contemplative experience and Christian spiritual perspective, he brought to the Western world a unique understanding of its need and condition and inspired others to turn inward as part of their own effort to understand and respond. In each of these ways Merton serves as a living and personal symbol of what this book aims to build toward: an understanding of education helpful in awakening and guiding us on our own journeys of the heart.

Merton personified a spirited Christian humanism that is often disavowed or undervalued in contemporary society for any of a host of reasons: general public wariness of religion, suspicion of the motives of clerical or church hierarchical authority, disagreement with religious doctrine, fear that the separation of church and state may be violated, or, more subtly, fear of one's own unbelief. Generally speaking, the substance and potential contribution of the Christian humanistic message is often neglected in the larger society because it is so often strictly associated with an institutional, religious source. There is no question that with Merton, however, Christian humanism had a genuinely personal voice.

"The center of Christian humanism," Merton assures us, "is the idea that God is love, not infinite power."[7] Merton's Christian humanism is thoroughly steeped in Christian spirituality and theology, and, most importantly, in his own inner experience. His writing testifies beautifully to this fact. What is especially significant in Merton's case, however, in addition to the quality of the essential message, was his unique ability to communicate it in a relevant and compelling way to a broad audience. Merton was able to speak from his Christian humanistic perspective to fundamental life questions and contemporary social issues. In large measure, he spoke from his own experience to the basic life experiences of his contemporaries in Western society, with special regard for their common historical circumstances. Merton wrote in the 1960s that "[Humanity] is in the midst of the greatest revolution [the] world has ever seen. This revolution is not merely political but scientific, technological, economic, demographic, cultural, spiritual. It affects every aspect of human life. . . . The great question is whether it can truly be directed to ends that are fully compatible with the authentic dignity and destiny of [humanity]."[8] Perhaps as much as anyone in his age, Merton endeavored to articulate and keep in clear view the human ends so easily forgotten in the midst of dramatic change. He spoke with strong conviction and passion for a deeper quality of human life, just as he often criticized sharply whatever he saw threatening it.

Merton felt that there was "a certain light which Christianity alone" could throw on "the most typical and most urgent problems of the modern world." In this vein he wrote that "Christianity can and must contribute something of its own unique and irreplaceable insights into the value of man, not only in his human nature, but in his inalienable dignity as a free person. The source of these insights is, of course, redemptive love."[9] This vision of love and the freedom and dignity of the person which Merton personified for so many, and which he articulated so well, provides the strongest impetus for this study. The substance of this vision and Merton's life speak eloquently, if not passionately, to the universal need to recognize who we are and to grow as whole persons, and thus to the subject of education.

What can one say about Thomas Merton on education? Merton spoke only sparingly of education. Compared to what we might hope to find, his direct commentary on the subject is frustratingly brief. Not unexpectedly, given the autobiographical bent of so much of his writing, much of this reflection is couched in personal narrative, a mode of expression not only typical and compelling for Merton but especially congenial to his subject since he discusses education in very personalistic terms. Even if considered as a whole, however, his thoughts provide only scattered kernels of insight; they want cultivation. Hence, after identifying them, the effort here is to nurture them with careful explication and elaboration.

It is difficult to separate a study of Merton's work from Merton himself. Particularly when the subject is education, Merton is wholly involved. A consideration of his life, as much as his thinking, is important in initiating the broader discussion. I have found it necessary and instructive, therefore, to go beyond the theme of Thomas Merton *on* education to explore its broader counterpart—Thomas Merton *and* education. I have aimed to develop a basic understanding of education in keeping with Merton's effort to enable others to recover the integrity of their own inner depths and his corresponding understanding of what it means to be a whole person. Necessarily, this has meant interpreting the meaning of education in the modern world in light of the Christian humanistic, spiritual perspective which Merton expressed so convincingly and through which he so often offered hope and insight for others.

What, in more specific terms, do Merton's life experience, his example and message, the geography of his life journey, if you will, suggest vis-à-vis the meaning of education? What, in turn, does this meaning provide for the educator?

As interpreted here, Merton's thought on education centers on two fundamental ideas, "the formation of the whole person" and "self-discovery." Both of these ideas have a particular meaning in the context of Merton's life and thought, more specifically in his sense of human existence, which means his understanding of the person in existential relationship with God. This understanding is not a matter of conventional theology for Merton but, above all, from his contemplative perspective, a matter of experience. Thus it has an empirical basis; yet, as a matter of interior and existential experience, rooted in the heart, one which is far removed from typical empirical investigation.

Many approaches to education gain popularity on the basis of widely acclaimed empirical study or because of the promise they hold forth for results in areas of public accountability. Some seek to model themselves on theories of how and why, developmentally, people think or behave the way they do. Whatever their validity or effectiveness as guideposts, however, few of these approaches or theories are rooted, as Merton's ideas are, in a spiritual sense of what it means *to be*, in the experience of "self" and "life" on the deepest existential level. Few, therefore, provide a perspective directly helpful in orienting one's sense of purpose or approach as it might pertain to the formation of the whole person understood from a distinctly spiritual point of view. Clarified in terms of their origin in an existential view of the person itself grounded in personal experience, Merton's ideas clearly offer such a holistic perspective.

When understood in terms of his basic grasp of what it means to be a person, Merton's ideas begin to convey a sense of the spiritual dimension of education. Challenged first and foremost, in conventional terms, is the sense in which both teacher and learner are considered as persons. Neither is simply a "what" to which can be added a measurable amount of knowledge and skill; nor is one in any explicit or implicit way the product engineer of the other. Their identity as persons, in a Mertonian sense, is much more relational in nature. Their existence in relation to each other, their world, and ultimately to God suggests a radically different consideration than either of these more narrowly defined notions imply.

Education understood to involve *formation* and *the whole person* implies an effort to foster an increased openness, attentiveness, and truthful responsiveness to a deeper reality and a deeper experience and understanding of the whole self. The educator becomes one who initiates and shepherds, or collaborates in, a process of awakening and of acquiring perspective, and, in some sense, of experiencing oneself whole. In so doing, the educator does not simply fulfill the commonly described role of "facilitator" with a new awareness. She or he must also become a genuine *participant*; for, if it is to link learning with the person (rather than have learning be the means or sign of becoming a person), if, again, it is to involve the whole person, the educative process must be grounded in a *shared* openness and a mutual personal regard. Thus the effort to teach, to enable and enliven, so evident in Merton's own example, needs to be disciplined by the very process it aims to foster. The process of teaching and learning can become a form of participation in the larger, ongoing effort to know and understand and live who we are spiritually as persons.

In order to build toward an understanding of an educative process which originates in and involves the whole person, we need to develop an awareness of person and personhood, of this "who we are." I have focused the next two chapters of the book on this question, exploring in Chapter 2 Merton's idea that education means "the formation of the whole person," and clarifying in Chapter 3 his related idea that the purpose of education is "self-discovery." I review in Chapter 2 various aspects of Merton's own life journey in building an understanding of "the formation of the whole person." Chapter 3 provides an interpretation of "self" and "person" in accordance with Merton's contemplative spirituality and Christian humanistic viewpoint. Subsequent chapters present a discussion of areas of personal growth (as suggested in Chapters 2 and 3) in and through which the formation of the whole person can be fostered, and which, therefore, can be taken into account in any process of education. These areas are identified as seeing, hearing, speaking, truthfulness, communication, and dialogue and are clarified in terms of Merton's life and work. Chapter 7 refers to Merton's experiences and example in developing broad characteristics of teaching relevant to "the formation of the whole person," teaching, therefore, which can be described as "person-oriented" or "personalistic." The final chapter offers a summary of the principal themes and key ideas linking the preceding chapters, as well as a concluding remark regarding the significance of Merton's educational ideas for our era.

Not unexpectedly, Merton challenges us to root our efforts in education in a firm spiritual ground and to consider education as an integral part of our lives as whole persons. Clarified in terms of his own life journey and his Christian spiritual and humanistic perspective, the meaning of his idea of education assumes an existential dimension that encompasses at once person and community, knowledge and wisdom. This perspective may prove helpful to the educator seeking to deepen a sense of personal vocation in education. It may also prove beneficial to the effort to orient one's educational intention and approach, in measuring and judging the value of educational activity, and in guiding the process of awakening and enlivening along the difficult journey that ultimately brings us home.

Notes

1. Thomas Merton, *The Seven Storey Mountain* (New York: Harcourt Brace Jovanovich, 1948).

2. Thomas Merton, "September 1968 Circular Letter to Friends," Appendix I, in *The Asian Journal of Thomas Merton*, ed. Naomi Burton, Brother Patrick Hart, and James Laughlin (New York: New Directions, 1975), p. 296.

3. Merton wrote extensively on contemplation and the monastic vocation; see especially *What Is Contemplation?* (Springfield, Ill.: Templegate, 1978), Chapters 1 and 2 in *New Seeds of Contemplation* (New York: New Directions, 1961), *The Monastic Journey*, ed. Brother Patrick Hart (Mission, Kan.: Sheed Andrews, and McMeel, 1977), and

"Marxism and Monastic Perspectives," Appendix VII, in *The Asian Journal*, pp. 326-343.

4. Merton, *The Monastic Journey*, p. 171.

5. Henry David Thoreau, *Walden* (New York: Bantam Books, 1962), p. 172. "Thoreau of course I admire tremendously," Merton wrote (Merton to Henry Miller, unpublished "Cold War Letters," #95, p. 157, Thomas Merton Studies Center, Bellarmine College, Louisville, Kentucky); hence, the comparison is not fortuitous. Merton mentions *Walden* in his journal *The Sign of Jonas* (New York: Image Books, 1953), p. 306, and Thoreau elsewhere, as, for example, in his essay, "Rain and the Rhinoceros," in *Raids on the Unspeakable* (New York: New Directions, 1966). I mention Merton and Thoreau again comparatively in the discussion of "Rain and the Rhinoceros" concluding Chapter 4.

6. Merton, "Monastic Experience and East-West Dialogue," Appendix IV, in *The Asian Journal*, p. 317.

7. Merton, "Christian Humanism," in Thomas Merton, *Love and Living*, ed. Naomi Burton Stone and Brother Patrick Hart (New York: Bantam Books, 1979), p. 134.

8. Ibid. I have substituted "humanity" for "man" in this quotation, as indicated by the brackets. Merton used the masculine pronoun extensively in his writing, and I have found it difficult to eliminate in quotation altogether what was a common practice for Merton without altering basic sentence structure. As in this case, I have made substitutions in some instances, in recognition of the limited perspective represented by the masculine pronoun; otherwise, I have retained Merton's original wording. In any event, Merton's awareness and appreciation of the feminine should not be overlooked, especially as manifested in his beautiful prose poem, *Hagia Sophia*.

9. Ibid., pp. 123-124.

2

The Education of
the Whole Person

Responding in 1968 to college student Mary Declan Martin's inquiry regarding his views on education, Thomas Merton wrote, "I believe education means more than just imparting 'knowledge.' It means the formation of the whole person."[1] Merton's reply represents one of the few instances in his writing in which he addresses the subject of education directly. Though unfortunately brief, his statement was the fruit of many years of written reflection and meditation on the meaning of "self" and "person." It captured as well the essence of his own commitment and experience in personal growth. Merton's understanding of education should be clarified and amplified first of all in these personal terms. This chapter begins that process by highlighting various aspects of Merton's personal growth, as suggested by his autobiographical and self-reflective writings, which help exemplify the meaning of "the formation of the whole person."

GEOGRAPHY OF A LIFE JOURNEY

The broad outlines of Merton's life story can be illustrated well through the metaphor of "journey." In fact, viewed as journey and in terms of the corresponding "geography" of time, place, and experience which journey implies, Merton's own personal life story presents ironic features whose explanation helps focus basic characteristics of his growth as a whole person, thus vivifying his central idea of what education means. Merton himself suggests the appropriateness of this metaphorical lens.

Merton's early autobiographical writing, represented especially by *The Secular Journal* and his celebrated *The Seven Storey
Mountain*, evinces his strong sense of life as journey.[2] Particularly in these early works, Merton tends to mark personal growth
through corresponding geographical images (primarily an im-
agery of place) rather than chronological reference. In *The
Secular Journal*, for example, written during the period just
prior to his decision to enter Gethsemani monastery in 1941,
Merton's spiritual insight and conviction to join the monks of
Gethsemani grow generally in correspondence with changes of
scene: from Perry Street in New York to Cuba, to St. Bonaventure College, to Gethsemani Abbey (for an Easter retreat), to
Harlem, and finally back to St. Bonaventure's just before entering Gethsemani as a novice monk.[3] The final passage of *The
Seven Storey Mountain*, published in 1948, similarly reveals Merton's acute sense of the correlation between the physical, geographical movement of his life and his understanding and an-
ticipation of his spiritual growth. In these closing words of his
autobiography, Merton relates what he hears of God's response
to his desire for solitude and closeness to God: "*But you shall
taste the true solitude of my anguish and my poverty and I shall lead
you into the high places of my joy and you shall die in me and find all
things in my mercy which has created you for this end and brought you
from Prades to Bermuda to St. Antonin to Oakham to London to
Cambridge to Rome to New York to Columbia to Corpus Christi to St.
Bonaventure to the Cistercian Abbey of the poor men who labor in
Gethsemani: That you may become the brother of God and learn to
know the Christ of the burnt men.*"[4]

The importance of the journey theme to Merton's understanding of his personal growth and in expressing his spiritual
aspiration to live in greater unity with God does not diminish
over time. In 1966, for example, Merton appropriately employs
the metaphor of movement while reflecting on his personal
experience of learning in his essay "Learning to Live": "I
[speak] from experience . . . as one who . . . has traveled
through various places of 'learning' and has, in these, learned
one thing above all: to keep on going."[5] During the period after
the publication of *The Seven Storey Mountain* in 1948, Merton
often expressed a desire to travel from the monastery of Geth-

semani or to relocate to places ranging from Latin America to Alaska.[6] He sensed in these places the potential for a deeper experience of solitude than he sometimes felt was possible at Gethsemani Abbey. Finally, in 1968, Merton's effort to keep moving resulted in actual long-term travel plans. His destination was Asia, chosen ostensibly in order that he might participate there in an intermonastic conference, but more importantly to stimulate movement in another sense. Merton hoped to deepen his understanding of his vocation by drinking from the wellsprings of Eastern monastic tradition.[7] This would be by far Merton's most extensive and significant physical journey while a monk of Gethsemani, just as it would prove to be his last.

The journey motif figures prominently in a "Circular Letter to Friends" that Merton wrote while coincidentally preparing for his trip to Asia. Geographically, however, Merton emphasizes a significantly new dimension: "Our real journey in life is interior: It is a matter of growth, deepening, and of an even greater surrender to the action of love and grace in our hearts."[8] "Place" and "journey" have to some extent become internalized for Merton. Indeed, "place," even as it refers to the monastery, has assumed a more spiritual identity.[9] Merton had written in his introduction to the Japanese edition of *The Seven Storey Mountain* in 1963 that "my monastery is not a home. It is not a place where I am rooted and established in the earth. It is not an environment in which I become aware of myself as an individual, but rather a place in which I disappear from the world as an object of interest in order to be everywhere in it by hiddenness and compassion."[10] Whatever may be made of Merton's search for more seclusion as a sign of physical restlessness, his increasing emphasis on the interior nature of his own life journey has to be taken into account as his deepest understanding of his own personal growth. It is revealing in this respect that in the very essay in which he discusses his learning in terms of movement Merton also asserts that "the graduate level of learning is when one learns to sit still and be what one has become."[11] In moving one has finally to discover who it is that is moving. Merton's trip to Asia reflected more this aspect of his interior journey than anything else. His presence in the world ultimately became a matter not of place but of "hiddenness and compassion" and would grow paradoxically in proportion to his physical and internal experience of solitude.

A more careful charting of the course of Merton's life journey through the transition between the mobility of his premonastic life and the stability of Gethsemani is revealing. While he was at Gethsemani, rooted in one physical "place," the "geographical" boundaries of Merton's life journey undergo paradoxically their most radical change.

Merton was born in Prades, France, in 1915.[12] He died accidentally, at age fifty-three, in Bangkok, Thailand, in 1968 during his Asian journey. During his lifetime he was schooled successively in France, England (Oakham public school and Clare College, Cambridge University), and the United States, where he received his M.A. degree in English from Columbia University in 1939. His self-guided travels included, most notably, sojourns in Italy and Cuba. Based on these facts alone, Merton's life journey seems to have been marked by a considerable geographical diversity. But the singular fact that he spent virtually his entire adult life in one place—Gethsemani Abbey—confounds this conclusion.

Merton entered Gethsemani Abbey on December 10, 1941, when twenty-six years old, only three years after his transforming and wholehearted conversion from an "atheist," as he considered himself, to Catholicism (he had been baptized a Christian as an infant, but religion did not play a formal role in his upbringing). He was a member of his Trappist monastic community for exactly twenty-seven years until his death on December 10, 1968. One of his singular religious commitments as a Trappist monk, in addition to silence, obedience, celibacy, and poverty, was to stability—stability in terms both of place and vocation. Although, as noted above, Merton often yearned for a monastic outpost with a guarantee of a more thorough solitude, his physical and vocational roots remained solidly with Gethsemani. As Father John Eudes Bamberger, one-time fellow monk and personal physician to Merton, has pointed out, Merton affirmed his Gethsemani commitment to his friends even while en route to Asia in 1968, saying, "I am a monk of Gethsemani and intend to remain one all my days."[13] By this time, however, Merton's vocation to greater solitude had been recognized by his community. In 1965 he was granted long-sought permission to live as a hermit on monastery grounds.

There is a strong overtone of paradoxical irony to the fulfillment of Merton's quest for deeper solitude as a hermit that compels explanation. It was while settling into the unassuming and more secluded lifestyle of the hermit that Merton's prominence in "the world" was peaking. Even as he sought to deepen his contemplative life—to open more space for his interior journey—his prophetic voice resounded more forcefully in the public conscience of his society. His potent writings on questions involving race, peace, and social justice (e.g., *Seeds of Destruction*), together with a growing correspondence, all testified to the irrepressible voice that rose from Gethsemani's monk of silence (see Chapter 5 for discussion of Merton's "social" voice).

During his period of monastic stability, then, Merton's interior journey covered an increasingly broader geographical expanse. In the place where he sought solitude with God his seemingly desultory youthful travels were transformed into a broad and compassionate identification with the oppressed and "marginal" of his fellow human beings; in the place of silence his voice more and more trespassed beyond the ostensible boundaries of vocational commitment and physical isolation.

What characterized this movement in Merton's life journey? What does it signify vis-à-vis his belief in education as "the formation of the whole person"?

FROM SEPARATION TO IDENTIFICATION: EMBRACING THE WORLD IN SOLITUDE

If one reads *The Seven Storey Mountain*, it is clear that Merton's understanding of education as "the formation of the whole person" cannot be genuinely understood without referring to his own personal experience of faith and solitude. Merton's autobiography illustrates dramatically that the most significant change in his young adult life (he was thirty-three at the time of its publication) pivoted on the fact of his growing faith and concomitant understanding and experience of solitude.

Merton underwent his gradual and joyful conversion to Catholicism at about the time that he began his graduate studies at Columbia University in 1938. During this transformation he was brought up, in his words, "by the kind Providence of God . . . from an 'atheist' . . . to one who accepted the full range and

possibilities of religious experience right up to the highest degree of glory."[14] On November 16, 1938, he was baptized in the
Catholic Church, thus liberating himself, in his mind, "from my
slavery to death."[15]

The sensation of freedom that Merton experienced upon
baptism was short-lived. He repudiated his conversion as more a
matter of intellect than a harmony of heart, mind, and will.
Thus it could only be considered vain, impoverished, and incomplete. Merton's struggle with the implications of this realization was expressed in part by vocational questioning. In seeking
the path toward more total conversion, he was drawn increasingly closer to the possibility of life in a formal religious community, recognizing at the same time the uncertain effect such a
decision would have on his deep vocational interest in writing.
In what would be his final entry in *The Secular Journal*, he
recorded his overwhelming conviction to materially " 'give up
everything' " and devote his life wholly to loving God.[16] He subsequently became a Trappist monk at the monastery of Gethsemani in Kentucky.

At Gethsemani, enclosed "in the four walls of my new freedom," Merton experienced "the Sweet Savor of Liberty."[17] His
entrance into the monastery was a fulfilling and momentous
event for him, yet one that he did not anticipate would bring
him closer to the world that he had presumably in good faith,
and with little misgiving, left behind.

By removing himself from "the world" Merton believed he
would most likely fulfill the spiritual promise of the life of
solitude for growing closer to God symbolized by Gethsemani.
The monastery at Gethsemani thus became *the* place, a new
geographical center, in some way a more real and certainly a
more transformative world than that manifested by the society
at large. It is in this vein that Merton wrote during his only visit
to Gethsemani prior to his becoming a Trappist: "This is the
center of America. I had wondered what was holding the country together, what has been keeping the universe from cracking
in pieces and falling apart. It is places like this monastery—not
only this one: there must be others. . . . This is the only real city
in America. . . . It is an axle around which the whole country
blindly turns, and knows nothing about it."[18]

The combined geographical and spiritual significance of the

monastery of Gethsemani for Merton is reflected in his poetry as well as his almost continuous journal writing. As Victor Kramer has pointed out, Merton's early poetry is replete with Gethsemani images illustrating a variety of spiritual themes.[19] His journal *The Sign of Jonas*, encompassing the years between 1946 and 1952, likewise focuses on Gethsemani, presenting his reflections on his life there and his growing understanding of solitude, self-knowledge, love, and a host of related topics.[20]

Merton also delved deeply into the roots of the monastic tradition represented by Gethsemani, eventually writing *The Waters of Siloe*, a history of the Cistercians, his own monastic order.[21] And, in order to learn more about the life of prayer and contemplation to which he had become dedicated, he avidly read the work of spiritual writers such as St. John of the Cross. Most importantly, he became steeped in the daily life of prayer, work, and ascetic practice which characterized his community's way of life.

Merton felt that he had established his right relation to Western secular society by removing himself from it in order to live in its unknown, silent "center" at Gethsemani. He was unequivocal in *The Seven Storey Mountain* in expressing his disillusion with, if not rejection of, the secular world and liberal in denouncing what he perceived as its shallow or warped sense of meaning and value. "When I wrote this book," he remarked in retrospect, "the fact uppermost in my mind was that I had seceded from the world of my time in all clarity and with total freedom. The break and the secession were, to me, matters of the greatest importance."[22]

In entering a Trappist monastery Merton became steeped in a centuries-old religious way of life and apprehended the world in strong, if not from some viewpoints mysterious, contrast to the Western world's most visible material aspirations and values. In adopting a contemplative mode of life he likewise set himself apart from modern modes of thought reflecting a view of God as a matter of psychological or sociological necessity, as a theological proposition, or as an unfathomable and unaccountable being remote from everyday life.[23] Nourished just prior to his Gethsemani years on a literary diet that included Etienne Gilson's *The Spirit of Medieval Philosophy*, Aldous Huxley's *Ends and Means*, and Christian spiritual classics such as Augustine's *Con-*

fessions, and Thomas à Kempis's *The Imitation of Christ,* Merton believed and, as suggested by his conversion, clearly experienced the reality of God's love and truth in his life.[24] As he recounts in *The Seven Storey Mountain,* "I became more and more conscious of the necessity of a vital faith and the total unreality and unsubstantiality of the dead, selfish rationalism which had been freezing my mind and will for the last seven years. . . . The only way to live was to live in a world that was charged with the presence and reality of God."[25]

Merton's aim in his newly chosen contemplative vocation was no less than to awaken his sense of "the presence and reality of God" in accordance with his love and will, and not simply his intellect. "What we have to learn is love," he wrote.[26] Hence the whole of Merton's personal existence, unlike that, presumably, of the secular majority, came to rest on the reality and experience of God's love.

Merton's disillusionment with his contemporary secular society and repudiation of his own role in the world prior to Gethsemani combined with his fervent faith, his vocational enthusiasm, and his nascent understanding of monastic purpose and tradition to cultivate his strong sense of separation from "the world." Yet even in his early monastic years separation did not mean total isolation. It is ironic that Merton spoke of his separated life of solitude through the very medium that maintained his essential link with the world—his writing. Particularly through *The Seven Storey Mountain* and his ongoing autobiographical writing represented by his journals, Merton kept the world abreast of the frustrations, confusions, uncertainties (among them, whether in fact to continue writing!), and glimmerings of truth which accompanied him on his interior journey.

Merton struggled painfully during his first decade of monastic life with the apparent contradiction between his urge to write and his vocational commitment as a contemplative. Not only would writing keep him in continued contact with the secular world he had to some degree forsaken (transforming him into a kind of secular personality), it might very well distract him in his life of prayer, worship, and manual work. Ironically, Merton's often intense ambivalence would be at least tentatively resolved in the very experience that he felt his writing might threaten: solitude.

Merton gradually came to realize that writing and the contemplative life were not necessarily mutually exclusive. His writing could play a helpful role in his contemplative life by providing a mirror in which to view his own honesty and integrity, and in this way become an integral part of the ongoing process of deeper and more total conversion.[27] At the same time, as the success of his own *The Seven Storey Mountain* suggested, his writing could invite others to reflect more deeply on their own interior life journey. By the year 1964 he could say, "Obviously, even writing is not excluded from a life of prayer."[28] It was important, however, that his writing, like anything else, be harnessed to his desire to do God's will; it was always subject to questioning in this respect.

Merton's eventual reconciliation of his desire to write and his vocation as a contemplative monk was reinforced by similar changes in how he experienced his relationship to the world and in how he understood the traditional boundaries of his vocation. As disclosed in his journals and essays, Merton gradually discovered a spiritual basis for a new relationship with the world. This spiritual foundation stood solidly beneath the disheartening veneer of Western secular society that he had rejected formally upon entering the monastery. He became aware of this more basic and intimate spiritual relationship with the world through his deepest experience of solitude.

Doubt and tension were not infrequent experiences in Merton's monastic life. For example, at the height of his anxious concern about whether his writing was appropriate to his contemplative vocation and his dismay at finding in solitude naught but his own weakness he wrote, "I am exhausted by fear."[29] Gradually, however, a new and rejuvenating experience of solitude supplanted his fear and preoccupations: "Solitude is not merely a negative relationship. It is not merely the absence of people. True solitude is a participation in the solitariness of God—Who is in all things. His solitude is not a local absence, but a metaphysical transcendence. . . . For us [monks], solitude is not a matter of being something *more* than other men. . . . For those who cannot be alone cannot find their true being. . . . Solitude means withdrawal from an artificial and fictional level of being."[30]

Merton's subsequent journal entry, on January 18, 1950, shows that he was able to integrate his urge to write into his

"participation in the solitariness of God." "My work is my hermitage because it is *writing* that helps me most of all to be a
solitary and a contemplative here at Gethsemani."[31]

Over time, Merton's deepening understanding of solitude as
"a participation in the solitariness of God" broadened his understanding and embrace of "all things" as a manifestation of God's
presence. To desire to know God more fully necessarily meant
loving all things in which God was. This would lead to the
realization of a deeper connection with all humanity, in which
God also was. In the experience of solitude Merton began to
discover a preexistent reality of being in which all subsisted and
which was distinguishable from the "artificial and fictional" level by which alone he had judged society and which had has-
tened his subsequent withdrawal from it. Merton assumed new
responsibilities in the monastery at about the same time that his
understanding and experience of solitude was changing. He
became "Master of Scholastics" in the early 1950s (providing
spiritual direction for those monks studying for the priesthood),
and beginning in 1955 he served for about ten years as "Master
of Novices." Particularly in this latter capacity, Merton played a
central role in the formative education of his fellow monks.
Together with his broadening experience of solitude, this increased responsibility for others in the monastery coincided
with another development for Merton: greater awareness of
and contact with "the world." Throughout the 1950s Merton's
vision widened to include more and more life outside the monastery.[32] His reading and correspondence expanded; he began
to discover his world anew.

It was after some "sixteen or seventeen" years at Gethsemani
(around 1957 or 1958), while on a medical trip to nearby Louisville, Kentucky, that the intimated lessons of solitude burst into
Merton's consciousness in a more concrete and transforming
way—at least this was his view in retrospect.[33] His journal account, refashioned for publication several years later in *Conjectures of a Guilty Bystander,* suggests the experience of an artist
who discovers transcendent beauty in the simple and ordinary:

> In Louisville, at the corner of Fourth and Walnut, in the center of
> the shopping district, I was suddenly overwhelmed with the realiza-
> tion that I loved all those people, that they were mine and I theirs,

that we could not be alien to one another even though we were total strangers. It was like waking from a dream of separateness, of spurious self-isolation in a special world, the world of renunciation and supposed holiness. The whole illusion of a separate holy existence is a dream. Not that I question the reality of my vocation, or of my monastic life; but the conception of "separation from the world" that we have in the monastery too easily presents itself as a complete illusion: the illusion that by making vows we become a different species of being, pseudoangels, "spiritual men," men of interior life, what have you.

Certainly these traditional values are very real, but their reality is not of an order outside everyday existence in a contingent world, nor does it entitle one to despise the secular; though "out of the world" we are in the same world as everybody else, the world of the bomb, the world of race hatred, the world of technology, the world of mass media, big business, revolution, and all the rest. We take a different attitude to all these things, for we belong to God. Yet so does everybody else belong to God. We just happen to be conscious of it and to make a profession out of this consciousness. But does that entitle us to consider ourselves different, or even *better*, than others? The whole idea is preposterous.

It is a glorious destiny to be a member of the human race. . . . A member of the human race! To think that such a commonplace realization should suddenly seem like news that one holds the winning ticket in a cosmic sweepstake.

This changes nothing in the sense and value of my solitude, for it is in fact the function of solitude to make one realize such things with a clarity that would be impossible to anyone completely immersed in the other cares, the other illusions, and all the automatisms of a tightly collective existence. My solitude, however, is not my own, for I see now how much it belongs to them—and that I have a responsibility for it in their regard, not just in my own. It is because I am one with them that I owe it to them to be alone, and when I am alone they are not "they" but my own self. There are no strangers![34]

The illusion of complete withdrawal from "the world," upheld so faithfully in *The Seven Storey Mountain*, was wholly shattered according to this retrospective account of Merton's Louisville experience. In Louisville Merton concretely experienced his fundamental relatedness to the world that he had once virtually forsaken and realized it gratefully as an experience heightened *in solitude*, and not in spite of it. He would later write confidently that "the first place in which to go looking for the world is not outside us but in ourselves. We *are* the world."[35]

Merton's experience on Fourth and Walnut was portentous. The "absurdities" and "mistakes" of the human race notwithstanding, he was now more fully implicated in the lives of the people of his world, if not fully identified with them "by hiddenness and compassion." And he had acquired a deeper, more inclusive understanding of solitude. If solitude was Merton's life, it was now more than ever everyone else's, too. He would express that understanding from his unique monastic viewpoint, at the same time that he would establish his own voice in the world.

Underlying the jubilation of Louisville, one senses a Merton more whole and especially more sure about the nature of his silent vocation in the midst of the world. He did not, by any means, underestimate his need for continued growth;[36] each successive self-understanding would be integrated into the whole to help pave the way for the next. Yet, his most mature thought on the subject of solitude seemed to follow in the heels of his Louisville experience. In "Notes for a Philosophy of Solitude," for example, published in *Disputed Questions* in 1960, Merton directly confronts a position that he might at one time have accepted: "The true solitary is not one who simply withdraws from society. Mere withdrawal . . . leads to a sick solitude, without meaning and without fruit."[37] Instead, the solitary seeks "a spiritual oneness in himself which, when it is found, paradoxically becomes the oneness of all men."[38] In "Love and Solitude," an essay written about six years later, he elaborates and amplifies this message: "The paradox of solitude is that its true ground is universal love—and true solitude is the undivided unity of love for which there is no number."[39]

Solitude, inasmuch as it attunes one to the world "charged with the presence and reality of God" and teaches one's fundamental relationship to others in love, becomes essential and necessary to an integrated and whole life. As Merton wrote: "It is all the more necessary, at this time, to rediscover the climate of solitude and of silence; not that everyone can go apart and live alone. But in moments of silence, of meditation, of enlightenment and peace, one learns to be silent and alone everywhere. . . . Solitude is not withdrawal from ordinary life . . . on the contrary [it] is the very ground of ordinary life. He who is truly alone finds in himself the heart of compassion with which to love not only this man or that but all men."[40]

Solitude had been Merton's teacher; "If you seek a heavenly light, I, Solitude, am your professor," he had written in the poem introducing *The Solitary Life*.[41] In listening to and learning from the experience of solitude, he had moved from a position of separation to one of compassionate identification with the world.[42] He would strive to be moved by naught but the love which solitude taught him, and which was the one essential ground of his identification, indeed "the very ground of ordinary life."

Merton's movement from separation to hidden and compassionate identification exemplifies a fundamental aspect of his growth as a whole person. Viewed from this perspective, it is clear that "the formation of the whole person" is not simply a matter of conceptual awareness and cognitive attainment, nor, in its interior dimension, merely a question of solitary introspection. It is rather personal growth on a level of concrete inner *experience* (solitude) which moves one toward deeper and more loving relationship and identification with others. It is a level of experience on which one gradually apprehends one's essential human quality in its *wholeness* and *inclusiveness*. It ultimately occurs on a level of existential experience profoundly more real than the "artificial" and "fictional" claims of society and thus serves as its own reason for confronting these claims.

Merton's life as a contemplative attuned him to growth on an existential plane of experience and awareness. The monastic life's discipline of prayer and work, meditation on scripture, spiritual writing, and Christian teaching were uniquely meant to foster such growth and to cultivate greater and greater openness to God and grace. Merton sought a more complete experience of solitude as a hermit in order to deepen that existential level of human experience and to live more fully, as it is inscribed above one Gethsemani portal, "For God Alone." As suggested by his account of his Louisville experience, however, it would be a mistake to consider such experience as the peculiar and sole province of the monk according to Merton's understanding.

Since solitude is "the very ground of ordinary life," to say that "the formation of the whole person" occurs in solitude is to suggest that it occurs on a level of experience which is deeply personal, accessible, and immediate, and which implicates all persons. To ask what education aimed at "the formation of the whole person" entails is to seek ways to make that level of experience more understandable, real, accessible, and meaningful for others.

As illustrated by Merton's own life journey, then, "the formation of the whole person" implies growth on a level of experience which opens and extends our relationship and identification with others even as it deepens self-understanding. It implies becoming increasingly aware of the reality and presence of God in our lives and our world through love. These implications of "the formation of the whole person" may themselves serve as landmarks by which to orient discussion of the quality of experience provided in education. They can help guide the process of discerning the quality of educational experience needed in order to open participants to experiencing life more on the whole existential level Merton discovered in solitude. Furthermore, they may lead to an exploration of the relationship between one's own interior journey and educational vocation. But the meaning of "the formation of the whole person" suggested by Merton's own personal experience can be broadened and deepened. The concepts of "self" and "person" are prevalent themes in Merton's spiritual writing. His understanding of them grew in correspondence with his personal growth. The next chapter strengthens the basis for understanding "the formation of the whole person" by providing an explanation of Merton's sense of "self" and "person" and his idea that the purpose of education is "self-discovery." It concludes by suggesting specific areas of personal growth on which education aimed at the formation of the whole person can focus.

Notes

1. Thomas Merton to Mary Declan Martin, April 1, 1968. (Though dated April 1st, Merton's letter is a response to Martin's letter of April 26th; May 1st is probably what Merton intended.)

2. Thomas Merton, *The Secular Journal of Thomas Merton* (New York:

Farrar, Straus & Giroux, 1959); Merton, *The Seven Storey Mountain* (New York: Harcourt Brace Jovanovich, 1948).

3. The *Secular Journal* is divided into five parts, each of which is titled according to one of the places mentioned.

4. Merton, *The Seven Storey Mountain*, pp. 422-423.

5. Merton, "Learning to Live," in *Love and Living*, p. 5.

6. See, for example, Thomas Merton, *A Vow of Conversation*, ed. Noami Burton Stone (New York: Farrar, Straus & Giroux, 1988), p. 45; and Michael Mott, *The Seven Mountains of Thomas Merton* (Boston: Houghton Mifflin, 1984), pp. 230, 270-271.

7. Merton, "November Circular Letter to Friends," in the *Asian Journal*, p. 320.

8. Merton, "September 1968 Circular Letter to Friends," in the *Asian Journal*, p. 296.

9. Even after almost twenty years there, Merton did not feel a strong relationship to Gethsemani as a physical place. "My place is in reality no place," he wrote to Jacques Maritain, "and I hesitate to act as if I were anything but a stranger anywhere, but especially here. I am an alien and a transient, and this is the last happiness that is possible to me: but a very real one." Merton to Jacques Maritain, February 22, 1960.

10. Robert Daggy, ed., *Introductions East and West: The Foreign Prefaces of Thomas Merton* (Greensboro, N.C.: Unicorn Press, 1981), p. 45.

11. Merton, "Learning to Live," in *Love and Living*, p. 4.

12. Facts about Merton's life are distilled from several sources, including especially his autobiography, *The Seven Storey Mountain* and Michael Mott's biography, *The Seven Mountains of Thomas Merton*.

13. John Eudes Bamberger, "The Monk," in *Thomas Merton / Monk, A Monastic Tribute*, ed. Brother Patrick Hart (Kalamazoo, Mich.: Cistercian Studies, 1983), p. 37. See also Merton's introduction to the Japanese edition of *The Seven Storey Mountain* in Daggy, ed., *Introductions*, p. 45.

14. Merton, *The Seven Storey Mountain*, p. 204.

15. Ibid., p. 221.

16. Merton, *The Secular Journal*, p. 270.

17. Merton, *The Seven Storey Mountain*, p. 372.

18. Merton, *The Secular Journal*, p. 183; cf., *The Seven Storey Mountain*, p. 325.

19. Victor Kramer, "Poetry as Exemplification of the Monastic Journey," in *The Legacy of Thomas Merton*, ed. Brother Patrick Hart (Kalamazoo, Mich.: Cistercian Publications, 1986), pp. 111-131.

20. Thomas Merton, *The Sign of Jonas* (New York: Image Books, 1953).

21. Thomas Merton, *The Waters of Siloe* (New York: Harcourt, Brace, 1949).

22. Daggy, ed., *Introductions*, p. 43.

23. For perspective, see Merton's comments on religion and religious fidelity in Thomas Merton, *Conjectures of a Guilty Bystander* (New York: Image Books, 1965), p. 154.

24. These books are all mentioned in *The Seven Storey Mountain.*

25. Merton, *The Seven Storey Mountain*, pp. 190-191.

26. Ibid., p. 372.

27. See, for example, Merton, *Vow of Conversation*, p. 29.

28. Ibid., p. 117.

29. Merton, *The Sign of Jonas*, p. 248; See also Henri Nouwen, *Thomas Merton: Contemplative Critic* (New York: Harper & Row, 1972), p. 46.

30. Merton, *The Sign of Jonas*, p. 262.

31. Ibid., p. 263.

32. See Merton's self-reflection in his introduction to *New Seeds of Contemplation* (New York: New Directions, 1961), pp. ix, x.

33. Michael Mott points out, from his vantage as the Merton biographer with authorized access to Merton's "restricted" work (including especially his journals), that Merton's account in *Conjectures* reflects a significant change from the original journal entry, written about five or six years earlier. The change reflects primarily a broader perspective on Merton's part; hence the actual transformational experience might not have been as profound as Merton's retrospective, meditative account suggests. See Mott, *The Seven Mountains of Thomas Merton*, pp. 311-312.

34. Merton, *Conjectures*, pp. 156-158.

35. Merton, "World," *Love and Living*, p. 106.

36. See, for example, Merton to Jacques Maritain, June 11, 1963: "There is yet work to be done in my own life. There are great illusions to be got rid of. . . . There is still much to change before I will really be living in the truth . . . without any more self-concern." In 1964, Merton wrote in his journal, "I am aware of the need for constant self-revision and growth." Merton, *Vow of Conversation*, p. 19.

37. Thomas Merton, "Notes for a Philosophy of Solitude," *Disputed Questions* (New York: Harcourt Brace Jovanovich, 1960), pp. 181-182; see also Thérèse Lentfoehr, "The Solitary," in *Thomas Merton / Monk*, pp. 68-69. Sr. Thérèse points out that Merton's "Notes" were drafted as early as 1955, with some elaboration by the time of their publication in *Disputed Questions* in 1960. It would be difficult to make a direct connection between Merton's Louisville experience and his publication of his "Notes" in 1960, especially given Mott's observation

that Merton's published account of his Louisville experience was written several years after it happened; what is clear, however, is Merton's maturing thought on solitude from the genesis of the "Notes" in 1955 to the Louisville experience several years later, to the publication of the "Notes" in 1960, to his Japanese introduction to *The Seven Storey Mountain* (August, 1963), to the rewriting of the Louisville experience for publication in 1965, and finally to his warm piece, "Love and Solitude" (1966), which, as Mott points out, reflects the influence of his love for "S," a nurse he met during that period.

38. Merton, "Notes for a Philosophy of Solitude," in *Disputed Questions*, p. 182.

39. Merton, "Love and Solitude," in *Love and Living*, p. 15.

40. Ibid., pp. 19, 21, 22.

41. Quoted by Thérèse Lentfoehr, "The Solitary," in *Thomas Merton/Monk*, p. 59.

42. Merton, "Preface to the Japanese edition of *The Seven Storey Mountain*, August, 1963," in Daggy, ed., *Introductions*, p. 43.

3

Self-Discovery as the Purpose of Education

Thomas Merton reflected and meditated deeply on the meaning of "self" and "person" along the path of his own interior journey. Much more than concepts, these terms denoted for Merton a profound existential reality which could only be understood fully through personal experience and love. He discussed them conceptually in his spiritual writings, however, in order to help himself and others better discern what was invariably a struggle to know in a more deeply personal sense who we are. Merton referred to this struggle as "self-discovery." Essentially, he meant the effort to discover ourselves as whole persons on the deepest existential and spiritual level.

"The danger of education," Merton wrote, ". . . is that it so easily confuses means and ends."[1] Merton held forth the idea of "self-discovery" as the one end of all education. For a person who experienced his own process of self-discovery in such a radical and transforming way, there could be no more meaningful end. Clarification of Merton's Christian contemplative view of self and person will help build a more full understanding of what he meant by this idea of educational purpose and help establish some of its implications for education aimed at the formation of the whole person. How, first of all, does Merton establish self-discovery as the purpose of education?

As noted in the previous chapter, Merton understood solitude to mean in part "withdrawal from an artificial and fictional level of being." One seeks instead a level of true being. Merton extends this idea into the realm of education when in his essay

"Learning to Live" he describes the basic purpose of education as "to show a person how to define himself [or herself] authentically and spontaneously in relation to his [or her] world." This process presupposes a basic freedom and understanding of self:

> The world is made up of the people who are fully alive in it: that is, of the people who can be themselves in it and can enter into a living and fruitful relationship with each other in it. The world is, therefore, more real in proportion as the people in it are able to be more fully and more humanly alive; that is to say, better able to make a lucid and conscious use of their freedom. Basically, this freedom must consist first of all in the capacity to choose their own lives, to find themselves on the deepest possible level. . . . The function of a university is, then, first of all to help the student to discover [him or her] self: to recognize [him or her] self, and to identify who it is that chooses.[2]

Merton subsequently declares that "the purpose of all learning" is "to dispose" people to have this basic self-discovery, in his words, to activate their "inmost center . . . [the] 'spark' which is my true self."[3]

Among the salient themes introduced in these selections from "Learning to Live," including freedom and fruitful relationship, self-discovery clearly has a pivotal status. The term reflects Merton's deep belief that the reality of human existence is found ultimately through an inner experience wholly one's own and moreover that it is through such experience alone that fully mature and authentic human being becomes possible. One's essential freedom is not realized in imitation of social status or standard or in accordance with any other externally imposed measure. Merton's message is clear: An education which would safeguard the personal capacity for free, creative, and genuine relationship with others in the world must ultimately provide for self-discovery.

Merton's view of the purpose of education as self-discovery is quintessentially "personalistic."[4] For Merton, the fruit of education is not a "what," whether that "what" is defined as a self measured in terms of academic degrees or a particular expertise, but ultimately "who." This "who" is not some ideal version of the "true self," that is, not an object for self-reflection, an image, or an abstract conceptual realization. Rather, it is the existential who, the whole person in existential reality, "the radical self in its uninhibited freedom."[5]

In keeping with its existential quality, self-discovery for Merton means more than a personal experience in the narrow sense of individual or separate. In fact, it has a broad communal dimension, implicated both in the paradoxical terms with which Merton often characterizes self-discovery and the concept of unity to which he often refers in describing it.

One must find oneself, Merton observes in *No Man Is an Island*, "in and through others."[6] This paradoxical prescription for self-discovery becomes more understandable when viewed as an indication of a dialectical pattern of growth involving self and others. This paradoxical, dialectical pattern is implicit in Merton's elaboration of the discovery process: "We cannot find ourselves within ourselves, but only in others, yet at the same time before we can go out to others we must first find ourselves."[7] The paradoxical nature of self-discovery also indicates, however, something more basic than a dialectical pattern of growth. It points to a deeper existential relationship in which self and other are united; only in this way can the paradox be understood.

In more ontological terms, the discovery of self in other entails the discovery of both in the common ground of existence or "being," God. To explain this ontological reality, Merton refers to the Christian existentialist belief which holds that persons share a life in common, in Christ; in the words of St. Paul quoted by Merton, "We are all members one of another."[8] In Merton's words, we are "members of a race which is intended to be one organism and 'one body.' "[9] This fundamental unity provides the basis for the formation of community and informs the self's understanding of personal difference in terms of complementarity and plurality rather than separateness and diversity.[10]

At the same time that it is deeply personal, then, self-discovery is inherently relational and communal. It also implies a dialectical pattern of growth involving self and others. As expressed in the language of Christian contemplation, these dimensions of self-discovery reflect discovery of Christ in oneself, and the corresponding discovery of oneself and others in Christ.[11] Expressed in more universal terms, they suggest the person as "one in the unity of love."[12] This theme will figure prominently in the more comprehensive discussion of person and community composing the latter part of this chapter.

It should be noted that the significance of Christian existentialist belief for discussion of self-discovery is not *specifically* in its theological validity. It lies, rather, for the purpose of this interpretation, in how it illuminates Merton's sense of the self or person for whose discovery education should aim. In this case, the doctrine of "the mystical body of Christ" illustrates both the source of Merton's understanding of self in relationship to others and the deep personal quality of that relationship. It provides as well an important basis for understanding how the concepts of unity and complementarity help to explain the meaning of self-discovery.

In general, the capacity of language to express the meaning of self-discovery is limited. The concepts of self, person, and community in particular evoke the personal and transpersonal qualities of self-discovery. Like the paradoxical mode in which Merton often expresses self-discovery, however, they are meaningful only insofar as they point to the "objective" yet "mystical" reality of existence on which self-discovery is predicated.[13] Merton was acutely aware of the limitedness of language and, moreover, of its power to mislead. As Merton points out in "The Inner Experience," "One may isolate the reality in a symbol, but then one must remember that it is not the symbol, and the symbol itself is incapable of communicating the full reality."[14] Failure to maintain this distinction between symbol and reality can easily result in misinterpretation of self-discovery as an ideology which is in some sense programable. Such a fabricated ideology would be antithetical to Merton's personalistic view of education and the spontaneous "freedom within" that self-discovery implies.[15]

Recognizing the limitation as well as the influence of language, one can proceed to more closely examine the concepts of self, person, and community as they are developed or implicated by Merton in his writing and as they help to elucidate the full, rich meaning of self-discovery as the purpose of education.

As described in "Learning to Live," the "true self" is "the mature personal identity, the creative fruit of an authentic and lucid search, the 'self' that is found after other partial and exterior selves have been discarded as masks. . . . This inner identity is not 'found' as an object, but is the very self that finds."[16] Subsequently, Merton writes that "learning to be oneself means . . . discovering in the ground of one's being a 'self' which is ultimate and indestructible."[17]

Three themes make these passages typical of Merton's writing on the self. Most prominent is the distinction made between an exterior (often the "external," "false," "empirical," or "ego-") self and inner (often "true" or "real") self. Less evident, but no less important, is the implied distinction between the self as "object" and the self as subject ("the very self that finds"). Association of the inner self with the "ground of one's being" constitutes another elemental theme. When examined in the context of Merton's contemplative philosophy, these themes offer valuable insight into the nature and characteristics of the self to be discovered through education.

"For man to be free," Merton asserts, "he must be delivered from himself."[18] In another instance, he writes that "in order to find myself I must go out of myself, and in order to live I have to die."[19] Not surprising vis-à-vis understanding Merton's work, the meaning of these statements derives more from their characteristically paradoxical nature than their actual language.[20] The contradictions they express cannot be reconciled except in terms of some deeper reality that they cannot directly convey or, put in another way, that they can intimate only by being contradictions. In some sense, then, their paradoxical nature is a witness to faith in something else, something "out of ourselves."[21] In this case, the "something else" is a self radically different from the self alluded to, a self which can be free, which can be found, and which lives. As William Shannon has pointed out, the found self is the "true self," and the lost self is the "exterior" or "false self."[22]

Much of Merton's spiritual writing is replete with references to the "false" and "true" selves, or their various synonyms.[23] It should be emphasized that Merton's distinction between the two is conceptual, not meant to imply that we in fact have a dual nature but more to illustrate the difference between an incomplete and more whole sense of existence; hence, they are important to differentiate here. Merton's words, written in 1966 after many years of reflecting on the "self," will help put this discussion in perspective: "I must . . . find my center not in an ideal self which just *is* (fully realized) but in an actual self which does all it can to be honest and to love truly, though it still may fail".[24] Often the false self serves as a kind of foil for its genuine counterpart. Its different manifestations, though more interrelated than discrete, can be grouped conveniently as psychological, social, and temporal in nature. Their explication will provide a rich counterpoint for discussion of the different manifestations of the true self.

THE FALSE SELF

Psychologically, the false self consists in witting or unwitting subjection to its drives and desires, convinced, in its self-centeredness, that they are the source of its existential reality.[25] It therefore mistakes the "individual and empirical ego" for the true self.[26] Responsible fulfillment of individual needs becomes the sole basis for self-realization and the predominate measure of its maturity.

According to Merton, the false self harbors a spurious view of reality because it prescinds from the spiritual basis in which alone the true self is found. "But when the outward self knows only itself," he offers, "then it is absent from my true self. It never acts according to the need and measure of my own true personality."[27] In his essay, "A Note on *The Psychological Causes of War* by Erich Fromm," Merton elaborates this point of view:

> The Christian concept of man . . . is one which sees man as a spiritual, or self-transcending being. That is to say that man . . . does not find his fulfillment or self-realization merely on the level of his own nature. . . . When our empirical ego is taken, without further qualification, as the true "person," the true "self," as the being who is the genuine subject of life, freedom, joy, and fulfillment . . . then we arrive at the most tragic frustrations and errors, because this implies a radical alienation of our true being.[28]

As exemplified in this passage, differentiation of the false and true selves clearly depends on distinguishing their corresponding psychological and spiritual origins.

In his essay "Rain and the Rhinoceros," Merton suggests that two of the strongest psychological attributes of the false self are its "fear of death and the need for self-affirmation."[29] The fear of death has temporal implications to be discussed below; the need for self-affirmation engages the self "in a futile struggle to endow itself with significance."[30] The false self thus acts as its own source of being and fulfillment; in terms of interaction, it is "challenging and defying . . . seeking either to dominate or to placate all that it confronts."[31]

In its psychological manifestations, the false self is maintained by pride, "a stubborn insistence on being what we are not and never were intended to be."[32] Merton develops this theme in *The New Man*: "Pride is a deep, insatiable need for unreality, an exorbitant demand that others believe the lie we have made ourselves believe about ourselves. It infects at once man's person and the whole society he lives in. It has as a secondary effect what theologians call concupiscence: the convergence of all passion and all sense upon the self. . . . It sees all things from the viewpoint of a limited, individual self that is constituted as the center of the universe."[33]

A singular irony is implicit in Merton's account of pride: It is precisely individual pride and self-centeredness which creates in society the collective illusion that in turn minimizes the self-satisfaction sought by the individual. Put in another way, the individual conforms and thus acquiesces to society both as a result and in spite of the self-centered compulsion of pride.[34] This is one way in which the "hidden drive to self-assertion"[35] which characterizes the false self is mirrored and magnified in the collective realm of society.

Merton lamented that "the world we live in has become an awful void, a desecrated sanctuary, reflecting outwardly the emptiness and blindness of the hearts of men who have gone crazy with their love for money and power and with pride in their technology."[36] As exemplified in this complaint, Merton often assesses the state of Western society in incisive, harsh, and uncompromising terms. He typically portrays Western society as a collective macrocosm of the individual by incorporating language characteristic of his descriptions of the false self. Thus, themes of willfulness and power recur in his observations, as in this passage from "Rebirth and the New Man in Christianity": "The West has lived for thousands of years under the sign of the Titan, Prometheus, the fire stealer, the man of power who defies heaven in order to get what he himself desires. The West has lived under the sign of will, the love of power, action, and domination."[37] Even more indicative of these themes, Merton writes in "The Contemplative Life in the Modern World": "The busy and impatient men of the West . . . seek, in a word, the triumphant affirmation of their own will, their own power, considered as the end for which they exist. Is not this perhaps the most foolish of all dreams, the most tenacious and damaging of illusions?"[38] Merton fervently and forcefully answers this question, distinguishing the illusory perceptions of the individual self, magnified in society, from the contemplative view of reality. This passage perhaps best illustrates Merton's understanding of the dynamic through which the false self's need for self-assertion achieves an aggregate effect:

> The contemplative way requires first of all and above all renunciation of this obsession with the triumph of the individual or collective will to power. . . . The aggressive and dominative view of reality places at the center the individual self with its bodily form, its feelings and emotions, its appetites and needs, its loves and hates, its actions and reactions. All these are seen as forming together a basic and indubitable reality to which everything else must be referred, so that all other things are also estimated in their individuality, their actions and reactions, and all the ways in which they impinge on the interests of the individual self. The world is then seen as a multiplicity of conflicting and limited beings, all enclosed in the prisons of their own individuality . . . all seeking to find a certain completeness by asserting themselves at the expense of others. . . . Thus there arises a spurious, inconclusive unity: the unity of the massive aggregate.[39]

The ethos of power and domination which results from the false self's need for self-assertion is thus maintained in a confusing web of impersonal, competitive activity. Inferentially, it is clear that this ethos, once created, has a reciprocal effect, sustaining itself by reinforcing the self-centered orientation of the individual. As Merton maintains, "When you say 'I think' it is often not you who think, but 'they'—it is the anonymous authority of the collectivity speaking through your mask."[40] He also makes clear that the alternative to this mutually destructive dynamic in which self and other are engaged involves "the contemplative way"—the way by which the wisdom of compassion, understanding, and love supplants "will."[41]

Just as the false self lives imprisoned in the illusory world created by its efforts at self-assertion, it is entrapped in its conceptualization and corresponding experience of time. This perspective is especially clear when Merton describes "Time and the Liturgy" in terms of the contrasting images of "the natural man" and "mass man."[42]

Merton states in his essay "The Inner Experience" that the false self is "the 'I' of temporal finalities."[43] It finds nothing redeemable about time. Viewed in terms of the seasons, time is a cycle whose renewal only promises death.[44] Viewed in a more linear sense, time is like the unceasing flow of a river; the false self is carried along helplessly in its current, concerned about the "lapse of time" or fearful of what lies ahead.[45] Consequently, the false self lives permanently uprooted from the present and the natural cyclical rhythm of life. Merton suggests that this unsettled state is a "linear flight from nothingness, a flight from reality and from God, without purpose and without objective, except to keep moving, to keep from having to face reality."[46]

Conditioned by its fear of death,[47] the false self regards time as an enemy.[48] Time is responsible for the calamitous ending to its life; because of time its superficial needs and desires will not ultimately be fulfilled. The false self anticipates no ultimate self-affirmation in death. Thus it exists in painful awareness of its transience, in continuous tension with time.[49]

In its "modern" guise, the false self endeavors to hide from time in the relentless pursuit of the contemporary; that is, it seeks relevance and identity by conforming to whatever is deemed currently "right."[50] "To be contemporary," Merton explains in " 'Godless Christianity' ?" "is to maintain one's place, to survive in the highly organized and breathless dynamism of the ephemeral. It is a kind of existentialism of fashion, in which there is no solid ontological ground of being, only the constant unpredictable flux of existence."[51] By living in this contemporaneous mode, the false self effectively inures itself to the cold, enemy hand of time.

This portrayal of the false self in relation to time, inasmuch as it is inferred from various references made by Merton, is somewhat overdrawn. This quality, however, may also be considered a measure of its validity. In keeping with Merton's general approach to discussing the self, it fulfills the instructional purpose of providing a vivid contrast and counterpoint for discussion of the life of the true self.

In flight from time, caught in a collective web of illusion woven by its attempts to fulfill a psychological need for self-assertion, and futilely engaged in establishing its identity over and against others in conformity to arbitrary external criteria of its own invention, Merton's false self constitutes a kind of mirage or anti-image vis-à-vis the true self. It thus provides perspective: Knowing what is counterfeit helps in distinguishing what is real as the "self." In so doing, it helps to clarify what Merton means by "self-discovery" as the purpose of education, and suggests fundamental areas of personal growth which can be fostered by education in the effort to dispose one for the personal breakthrough that is self-discovery.

THE TRUE ("REAL" OR "INNER") SELF

The true self embodies a consciousness and orientation to reality wholly different from its false counterpart. While this difference can be delineated comparatively in terms of the psychological, social, and temporal manifestations of the false self, it can only be understood fully as something much more fundamentally whole and unified than these distinctions imply. To the extent that this difference is clarified, the purpose Merton identifies for education will be better understood. Toward that end, this section focuses on establishing and explicating the qualities, manifestations, and characteristics of the true self.

In *Day of a Stranger*, a personal essay to Latin American friends, Merton writes, "In an age where there is much talk about 'being yourself' I reserve to myself the right to forget about being myself, since in any case there is very little chance of my being anybody else."[52] This self-effacement reflects Merton's own effort to eschew identification in terms relevant to the false self.[53] In characterizing himself as "a stranger," Merton was stating that his identity existed outside the realm of society, that is, outside the realm of "multiplicity, activity, incompleteness, striving, and desire."[54] Thus he was expressing his intention to live simply as who he was in his reality as a whole, undifferentiated being, that is, in the eyes of God.

The false self lives divided, identifiable in such individual fragments as body, soul, personality, mind, and social image. In contrast, the true self is indivisible, the self in its totality, integrated.[55] The false self tends to identify itself in terms of its external activity, its output; it must be engaged in doing something in order to experience itself as real. The true self simply is. It does not have to do in order to be, though in being it is quite capable of doing. The difference is that its doing is motivated by love, reflected in the quality (not quantity) of its actions.[56]

Much more than *an* experience, which implies a self considering itself, the true self is the lived experience of its own wholeness.[57] Therefore it does not possess itself either as an idea or an image. Put in another way, the true self, unlike its self-conscious counterpart, is a lived consciousness, rooted in its actual being.

The true self is real for Merton precisely because it cannot be self-constructed—a being cannot endow itself with life. Rather, and with the profoundest of implications vis-à-vis the reality of the true self—life has been given to it. Therefore, in contrast to the illusory life that the meaning-making false self is devoted to creating, the life of the true self is free.[58] At the same time, recognizing the source of its being outside itself, it is conscious of its fundamental connectedness to all living beings. Therefore, the true self does not assert itself over and against the world as object, nor does it seek to possess the world.[59] Its consciousness is more of wholeness and unity; in what Merton calls "a kind of ontological openness," it apprehends the world more as a living expression of being, of love, of God.[60]

In "The Inner Experience," Merton describes the true or "inner self" as "our entire substantial reality itself, on the highest and most personal and most existential level. It is like life and it is life. . . . It is the life by which anything else in us lives and moves. It is in and through and beyond everything that we are. If it is awakened, it becomes a living awareness of itself; and this awareness is not so much something that we have, as something that we are. It is a new and indefinable quality of our living being."[61] As depicted in this passage, the true self is a dynamic fusion of what is common—"life"—and what is unique or "most personal"—the individual person. In "Learning to Live," Merton refers to this dynamic quality of the true self as "a fusion of freedom and unfreedom, being and unbeing, life and death," and as a "spark," an "event," and an "explosion."[62] True self-realization is a creative, life-affirming event in which the self and its life-giving source meet.

The dynamic metaphors that Merton uses to describe self-discovery suggest its mystical quality. Viewed from a Christian spiritual perspective, this signifies, on one level, an experiential awareness of the indwelling presence of Christ, and, on another, mystical union with God, the source and ground of all being.[63] For Merton, the ultimate significance of this event can only be understood from this perspective. However, he does not consider it exclusively in this way.

Precisely because it denotes for him a living reality, Merton was able to enlist a rich language—replete with metaphors such as "life," "consciousness," "freedom," "love," and "presence"—to describe self-discovery.[64] In *Zen and the Birds of Appetite*, Merton confirms the validity of this "nonmetaphysical way" of expressing the ontological reality which is the true self.[65] This question of validity needs to be addressed in order to make the idea of self-discovery, and its significance as the purpose of education, as understandable and accessible as possible. To limit discussion of the true self to theological terms, or, conversely, to preclude discussion because of the true self's theological import, is to proscribe it in a way that Merton certainly did not and mistakenly to consider it less in terms of a lived reality than as a matter for conceptual debate. While the language Merton uses to describe self-discovery may be distinguishable, and importantly so, as metaphysical or nonmetaphysical, and theological or nontheological, only when understood in its Christian spiritual meaning is the deeply personal nature of self-discovery fully conveyed.[66]

Reflecting its mystical quality, the true self is discovered wholly in a loving personal encounter, the person in existential contact with God, the source of life.[67] "Encounter," in this context, hardly denotes a chance meeting; rather, it refers to direct, concrete experience of the infinite and eternal presence of God in oneself, and of one's being in God.[68] It is a living recognition of the contingent reality of one's life in the unlimited expanse of God's love, and a simultaneous recognition of that reality for everyone else—with whom one is fully identified in unity and love. In the language of Christian contemplative spirituality, the true self is fully identified with Christ, living "in" or "as" Christ, just as Christ is present in the true self.[69] Likewise, in contrast to the self-limited terms of the false self, others are seen as co-persons in Christ.[70] In its power to radically transform one's consciousness and orientation to reality, this personal encounter is no less than an "explosion" for Merton.[71] One sees from an entirely new viewpoint.[72] The false self's arena of activity is replaced by a new landscape; reflecting personal relationship with Christ, one stands in a new relationship with persons and the material world.[73] Yet, precisely because it reflects true and real identity, this new vision and relationship has an old, ordinary quality as well. As Merton says in his chapter on "Realism in the Spiritual Life" in *Life and Holiness*, "paradoxically, on this new level we recover our old, ordinary selves. . . . The 'new man' is totally transformed, and yet he remains the *same person*. He is spiritualized . . . in Christ."[74] In personal identification with Christ, the true self is enabled to live more "awake," more simply, and more fully in the concrete, everyday world.[75] Put in another way, the true self embraces the great gifts of freedom and love in its everyday life. The dynamic, radical change which the true self represents can only be fully understood as an inner, enlivening, and personalizing experience, involving the individual person and the person of Christ.[76] Actualized as person, thus conscious of the living unity of all persons in Christ, the true self is able to see and relate to the world in its personal, *subjective* reality.

Merton often distinguishes the true and false selves in terms of their subject-object orientation.[77] The false self, in the extreme, regards persons and things equally, in proportion according to its own needs. The false self knows only what it can prove to itself. Its knowing is an act of self-reflection, if not self-ingratiation; it only holds forth as meaningful what it can tell itself. It thus limits its interaction with the world (implying nature as well as people), in the extreme manipulating it to its own image, less dramatically, viewing the world as an obstacle course of objects that it must successfully negotiate. It does not view truth as a reality that can be experienced on any level deeper than its own self-defined "reality," in accordance with its unmitigated efforts at "self-assertion" and "self-affirmation."

The true self, on the other hand, stands in relation to objects more as they are, or, more accurately, allows them to be and to mean what they are.[78] By virtue of its inner orientation, therefore, it enters into a wholly different qualitative relationship with the external world. Similarly, in what can be described as a *true self to true self* relationship, the true self identifies with persons as subjects.[79] Relationship for the true self is thus inter-subjective in nature. It lives in awareness of the mutual subjectivity and complementarity of persons; put in another way, in awareness of existential unity and complementary uniqueness.[80]

The true self's world becomes personalized and relationship subjectified through love. In his most relevant and illuminating essay on this topic, "The Power and Meaning of Love," Merton explains the dynamic and effect of this essential way of relating: "Love brings us into a relationship with an objectively existing reality, but because it is love, it is able to bridge the gap between subject and object and *commune in the subjectivity of the one loved*. Only love can effect this kind of union and give this kind of knowledge-by-identity with the beloved."[81] Subjectivity clearly does not refer here to the self-aware or ego-centered experience that Merton suggests elsewhere dominates the modern, Cartesian-inspired consciousness. Quite otherwise, it refers to the whole subjective reality of the self in a communion of personal love.[82]

Two fundamental characteristics of the true self are set in relief by this discussion of its subjective nature. The first is its deeply personal quality, in which all others are implicated as subjects, because all subsist in the personal love of God. Second, just as it ultimately enters into personal relationship through subjective identification, the true self views the world of objects in a direct, unprejudiced way; or, rather, it simply sees things as they are. In "The Inner Experience," Merton characterizes this way of seeing as "direct knowledge," a kind of simple apprehension of the truth of things.[83] Thus, self-discovery implies not only an ontological reality, but an epistemology that stands in direct contrast to the way of knowing of the false self—whose knowledge of the world, and relationship to others is mediated, in varying degrees, by its efforts at self-affirmation. If it is to nurture the growth of the true self, education clearly will have to nourish a subjective experience of knowing. Education driven solely by a view of knowledge as a matter of discrete and objective, if not manipulable, entity will provide little support for true self-discovery. Such education habitually removes knowledge from the realm of personal experience and connectedness to the world. It fails to enhance one's sense of reality and is thus lifeless.

It is not possible within the scope of this discussion to provide a full analysis of Merton's understanding of psychological development in relation to the true self. So it would be difficult to establish a strong foundation for discussing how education, in providing for particular aspects of psychological development, might fulfill the purpose of self-discovery. Since, however, this was a topic of important personal and intellectual concern for Merton, and one which bears significantly on this effort to explain self-discovery, it is appropriate to address it in a general way here.[84]

Merton establishes firmly that the true self is in no sense a psychological self-realization.[85] The true self simply is not identifiable in psychological or empirical terms. It is not the looked-for result of some process of psychological adjustment in which the ego or empirical self may.or may not play a prominent role; nor does it imply a distinct self which has found or attained to something it can identify as part of itself.

Whereas self-realization for the false self would entail fulfillment of its psychological need for self-affirmation and will to self-assertion, "true" self-realization entails inner discovery of the "someone that one already (potentially) is, the person one is truly meant to be";[86] that is, "the very self who finds."[87] The interior, spiritual nature of the true self precludes psychological definition or explanation.[88] As explained earlier, the true self lives in personal awareness of its ontological source of being in God and in the "unity of love" in which it is fully identified with others.[89] Its life, therefore, is moved by the love which creates the bonds of its relationship to God and others.

At the same time, however, that he emphasizes the fundamental difference between psychological self-realization and self-discovery, Merton enthusiastically affirms the importance of paradigms of psychological growth which implicate qualities and characteristics of the true self. For example, in a letter to Erich Fromm, the well-known philosopher and psychoanalyst, Merton expresses his total agreement with Fromm's thesis on the humanistic conscience and its central themes of freedom and responsibility; he specifically notes its basic compatibility with Christianity.[90]

Merton makes a similar comparison in his essay, "Final Integration—Toward a Monastic 'Therapy,' " in which he reviews the work of Reza Arasteh, a psychoanalyst.[91] In particular, he delineates those qualities which Arasteh attributes to the fully integrated personality that can also be considered hallmarks of the "saint" (essentially, the true self). Included among them are a transcultural consciousness, a deep inner freedom, and "a deeper, fuller identity than that of [the] limited ego-self which is only a fragment of [one's] being."[92] Merton also notes that one who has achieved the psychological integration that Arasteh describes "apprehends . . . life fully and wholly from an inner ground that is at once more universal than the empirical ego and yet entirely his [or her] own . . . is in a certain sense identified with everybody. . . [and] is guided not just by will and reason, but by 'spontaneous behavior subject to dynamic insight.' "[93] While recognizing the full correspondence of these characteristics of psychological integration with those of the true self, and their importance to the well-being of society, Merton points out the significant difference of their psychological and spiritual origins.

Merton's comparison of psychological growth and self-discovery, especially as represented in his essay on final integration, is instructive. It indicates first of all his commitment to making self-discovery as broadly comprehensible as possible, particularly in light of the propensity of his society to posit personal identity in psychological terms. Second, it indicates his belief that many of the characteristics of the true self are approximated at the highest level of psychological maturity and expands the conceptual language with which characteristics of the true self can be described. In particular, Merton shows that he is at ease with "integration," "transcultural," and "universal man" (implying an inclusive consciousness rather than any kind of cultural homogeneity) as concepts which can be applied in a discussion of the attributes of the true self.

Merton's comparison does not make clear how growth to

psychological maturity might be related to actual self-discovery. In his preface to *No Man Is an Island*, Merton does suggest that self-discovery, as a salvific event, "to some extent presupposes, and usually effects and always transcends" psychological self-realization.[94] Similarly, in his final integration essay, he mentions that the maturity evident in the "saint" "normally includes the idea of complete psychological integration."[95] The fact that Merton does not identify a causal relationship between psychological maturation and self-discovery underscores his belief that self-discovery is exclusively a spiritual event, encompassing the full reality of the self; therefore, it cannot possibly be enacted within the confines of the psychological realm.

In *New Seeds of Contemplation*, Merton states that "I must look for my identity somehow, not only in God but in other men."[96] In *No Man Is an Island*, as noted earlier, he suggests that one must find oneself "in and through others."[97] Echoing these thoughts, he concludes in "The Inner Experience" that "it is probably safe to say that no man could arrive at a genuine inner self-realization unless he had first become aware of himself as a member of a group—as an 'I' confronted with a 'Thou' who completes and fulfills his own being."[98] Taken together, these insights point to a central aspect of Merton's understanding of self-discovery—that it is founded on relationship. "One must not forget," he counsels in "Learning to Live," "the dimension of relatedness to others."[99]

Merton characterizes Western society, built in the image of the false self, in terms of power, aggressiveness, multiplicity, and division. Members of society exist atomistically, as anonymous individuals or "mass-men";[100] the society exists as a disunited aggregate or "collectivity."[101] This "mass society," in Merton's estimation, "is constructed out of disconnected individuals—out of empty and alienated human beings who have lost their center and extinguished their own inner light in order to depend in abject passivity upon the mass in which they cohere without affectivity or intelligent purpose."[102] Merton's message is clear: There is no "ground," no identity in mass society beyond its own created, mesmerizing, and stultifying illusions.

The true self, enabled by love to enter into relationship with its whole, subjective being, helps move society from the realm of individual anonymity to a realm of personal identity;[103] and from the realm of collectivity to the living and fruitful realm of community.[104] As recorded in *Conjectures of a Guilty Bystander*, Merton's retrospective account of his experience in Louisville at "the corner of Fourth and Walnut," filled with the joy of recognition, indicates his own concrete awareness of the personality of self and society: "I was suddenly overwhelmed with the realization that I loved all those people, that they were mine and I theirs, that we could not be alien to one another even though we were total strangers."[105] In what might be termed the humble voice of self-discovery, Merton adds,

> It is a glorious destiny to be a member of the human race. . . . There is no way of telling people that they are all walking around shining like the sun.

> Then it was as if I suddenly saw the secret beauty of their hearts, the depths of their hearts where neither sin nor desire nor self-knowledge can reach, the core of their reality, the person that each one is in God's eyes. If only they could all see themselves as they really *are*.[106]

Only from a consciousness that understands who persons "really are," that is, understands the "invulnerable inner reality"[107] or "spark" in which personal identity is realized,[108] can the relationships necessary for building a fully personalized and therefore a more genuinely communitarian society be formed.

Unlike the false self, whose will to self-assertion defines its relationships, the true self does not seek to control or dominate others as "object." Rather, it identifies with them as subjects, thus sharing in the subjectivity which is intrinsic to them both, and which signifies the loving presence of God in which they both subsist. Recognizing this significance, the true self seeks to create a dialogue with the other that will enable both to "listen" and respond more fully to love. This is what Merton calls "person-oriented" thinking. He introduces this theme in the context of a discussion on Christian nonviolence.[109]

The principles and philosophy of Christian nonviolence, which Merton explores in, among others, his essays "Blessed are the Meek" and "Gandhi and the One-Eyed Giant," offer an especially rich perspective on the nature of true self relationships.[110] Inasmuch as it is predicated on a fundamental respect

for the human person, and thus faith in the spiritual identity
common to all persons, the nonviolent approach aims to allow
others to develop their own inner response to a situation.[111]
Dialogue thus involves mutual understanding of personal subjectivity and loving response. Merton explains: "'Person-oriented' thinking . . . does not seek so much to *control* as to *respond*,
and to *awaken response*. . . . All it seeks is the openness of free
exchange in which freedom and love have freedom of action."[112] Merton thus indicates a particular quality of relationship as the basis for the true self, a quality accentuated in the
context of nonviolent response. The true self, in its humility
and corresponding vulnerability, acts as a witness to and catalyst
for awakening a sense of truth.[113] This posture, as Merton
suggests, is an outgrowth of the true self's orientation to the
basic unity of persons in love.[114] In this way, the true self seeks
to help others discover the loving unity in which it lives. To
understand self-discovery as the purpose of education, then, it is
clear that it must be considered as inseparable, in a very concrete sense, from "other-discovery." Self-discovery, in a word, is
relational in nature.

Unlike the false self, the true self does not exist in fundamental tension with time. It does not live in fear of the inevitability
of death; therefore, it does not perceive struggle with time as an
enemy whose final victory is certain. Its life does not consist in
the futile activity of asserting its will over and against its own
mortality. In conventional temporal terms, the true self orients
its life to the present—"The present is our right place," writes
Merton.[115] In more Christian spiritual terms its life is oriented
to "presence," to the actual, near, living presence of God[116]—as
Merton notes, the "actuality of God's presence is something that
does not belong to the past or to the future but only to the
present."[117] Since it is oriented to "presence," time for the true
self is "utterly transparent."[118] Put in another way, living in the
presence of God means, for the true self, living in the "fullness"
of time,[119] in God as the alpha and omega, the beginning and
end. Thus, time is not, as in the terms of the false self, either a
means or a deterrent to an end, but a living fulfillment of the
end.

Merton's understanding of the true self's relation to time is
deeply rooted in his Christian eschatological vision. "The Chris-

tian 'present,' " he explains, "has something of the character of eternity in which all reality is present at once."[120] In the *present* is the eternal and abiding *presence* of Christ.[121] The true self's relationship to time also reflects the personalism inherent in self-discovery. Orientation to the present is orientation to a deeply personal reality; in contrast to the restlessness of the false self, it implies living rooted in the "ground of being." Self-discovery, then, implies what Merton calls in his journal *The Sign of Jonas* "sinking into the heart of the present."[122] The true self is in a sense freed from fundamental concern about time. It lives not *for*, but in the moment.

Broader understanding of the present-orientation of the true self is closely linked to the vivid metaphors of "awake" and "aware" to which Merton's explanations of discovery of the true self often defer.[123] In *Raids on the Unspeakable*, for example, Merton writes: "To have an identity, [the individual] has to be awake, and aware. But to be awake, he [or she] has to accept vulnerability and death . . . for the sake of the invulnerable inner reality which we cannot recognize (which we can only *be*) but to which we awaken only when we see the unreality of our vulnerable shell."[124] In this context, awakening denotes an opening up of the whole self to its personal, existential identity. It in this sense implies awareness of the "presence" of love, of God, in its life. Thus the metaphors "awake" and "aware" help to describe the true self's relationship to time.

The life of the true self is nothing but concrete and real for Merton. At the same time, however, metaphors such as "awake" and "aware" fulfill the important purpose of evoking particular qualities of that life. "Awake" and "aware" implicate the life of the true self in the presence of God's love. They suggest, in particular, attitudes of receptivity, openness, and listening—not only to "presence" in an interior sense, but to "presence" as manifested in the lives of others and in the natural world. And this presence, tantamount to life itself, is alive, vivifying, even playful.[125] Merton beautifully portrays the presence of God as a "cosmic dance": "For the world and time are the dance of the Lord in emptiness. The silence of the spheres is the music of a wedding feast. . . . We are invited to forget ourselves on purpose, cast our awful solemnity to the winds and join in the general dance."[126]

Viewed in comparative perspective, the meaningfulness of "awake" and "aware" as metaphors which illustrate the life of the true self appears strengthened. The Buddhist concept of "mindfulness," whose clarification Merton sought in a final intellectual and spiritual odyssey in Asia, provides one basis for comparison.

In the words of Bhikkhu Khantipalo, "Mindfulness is the awareness of what one is doing while one is doing it, and of nothing else."[127] According to Bhikkhu, one who is mindful has "brilliant awareness of *NOW* all the time."[128] At least in Bhikkhu's conceptual terms of "awareness" and "*NOW*," mindfulness has a clear analogy to "awake" and "aware." In meaning, however, they seem more compatible than congruous, most obviously because the "NOW" of mindfulness does not evoke the "presence" implicit in wakefulness. While clearly needing further study, the apparent compatibility of these concepts helps broaden understanding of what the true self's capacity to live rooted in the present means.

As compelling and potentially of greater relevance to an understanding of "awake" and "aware" is the concept of "attention." Simone Weil, philosopher, mystic, and teacher, develops this concept in her essay "Reflections on the Right Use of School Studies with a View to the Love of God."[129] "Attention," she writes, "consists of suspending our thought, leaving it detached, empty, and ready to be penetrated by the object. . . . Above all our thought should be empty, waiting, not seeking anything, but ready to receive in its naked truth the object that is to penetrate it."[130] The openness ("empty, waiting") and receptivity ("ready to receive") which characterize "attention" in this explanation recall these same characteristics in the awareness of the true self. The living quality Weil attributes to "object" is even more comparatively striking, evoking the true self's openness to "presence." Weil's explanation of this living quality confirms the basic connectedness of "attention" and "awake" and "aware": "Being a little fragment of particular truth, it is a pure image of the unique, eternal, and living Truth."[131] Weil's "living Truth" can be considered tantamount to the "presence" of God.

The meaningfulness of this basic comparison of attention with qualities of the true self lies not only in the broader view of self-discovery that it provides but also in the concrete perspective that it begins to build on how this purpose of education might be fulfilled. Weil links attentiveness and school study with the apprehension of a deeper truth. Merton similarly suggests that study—the effort to know the truth about something—can prepare the way for "serious reflection" or meditation and thus for more concrete experience of the deepest realities of life.[132] He also points to the importance of attentiveness in other areas of everyday life: "In solitude . . . one must attend carefully to everything. If you apply yourself carefully to what you do, great springs of strength and truth are released in you. If you drift or go inattentively . . . the strength turns against you."[133] These views strongly suggest the significance of attentiveness to the formation of the whole person and thus its importance as an area of further study for education.[134]

PERSON AND COMMUNITY

As explained and interpreted thus far, self-discovery clearly refers to the dynamic, simultaneous discovery of one's own identity and the identity of all in a single, living, loving, deeply personal unity with God. Less clear, but hardly less significant, is what self-discovery enables one to become—a person. "And what is the person?" Merton asks. "Precisely," he answers, "[the person] is one in the unity which is love."[135] In a word, the person is the human manifestation of the love of God, the true self uniquely animated in love. Just as "love," for Merton, is the "key to the meaning of life,"[136] it is the key to understanding what he means by person. The person subsists in love; the life of the person is determined in and by love. "Our whole life," Merton relates, "is a participation in that cosmic liturgy of 'the love which moves the sun and the other stars.' "[137] Love, then, is not a self-contained emotional quality harnessed to the wishes of the false self. It is rather the all-embracing, all-pervasive essence of God, present in all things and everyone, the sole motive and actualizing force of the person.

To live in the unity of love implies both solitude and relationship. The person becomes attuned to the presence of God and the existential wholeness of the true self in the solitude of silence—in the inviolate interior space inaccessible to the influence of the collectivity or the vagaries of the false self.[138] Neither solitude nor silence, however, indicates isolation (the condition of the false self). As Merton emphasizes in *The Way of Chuang Tzu*, the person is realized only in relationship.[139] Thus, personal relationship reflects, however imperfectly, the fundamental spiritual unity of all persons in God, and the personal relationship of each person with God.[140] For Merton, the "other" is realized in solitude, just as the true self is realized in the other (that is, in relationship). In other words, the growth of the person occurs dialectically, the unique and common identity of both finally realized in "the unity which is love."[141]

Self-discovery, as the discovery in which one's full identity as a person is realized, is clearly a discovery of love in Merton's view, but love understood as an expression of the infinite depths of God's being intimately present in all life and uniquely reflected in the human capacity to love. Considered from this perspective, Merton's concept of person cannot be confused with secular humanistic or libertarian formulations which posit the growth of the person in such terms as freedom, responsibility, and integrity. At the same time, Merton's idea of person to some extent presupposes humanistic criteria for personal maturation, Merton acknowledging, in fact, a fundamental congruence of meaning and significance for these terms as used in secular or Christian humanistic contexts. Considered *apart* from this perspective, Merton's idea of person in reality becomes something likewise apart, a single, isolated entity disembodied from its true existence in ontological unity and relationship.

Merton was fully aware that the love of which he wrote, though fully present and accessible to all, was not easily discovered in a society habitually diverted from the life of the inner or true self and the silence and solitude in which alone it could be recognized and understood.[142] As he concludes in "Christianity and Totalitarianism," "Love cannot exist except between persons. For there to be love, we must first of all safeguard the liberty and integrity of the human person. We must provide an education that strengthens man against the noise, the violence, the slogans, and the half-truths of our materialistic society."[143]

In a passage from *Thoughts in Solitude*, Merton amplifies those qualities that need to be safeguarded in order to ensure the growth of the person—and society—in love: "To be a person implies responsibility and freedom, and both these imply a certain interior solitude, a sense of personal integrity, a sense of one's own reality and of one's ability to give [oneself] to society—or to refuse that gift."[144] Merton's message is clear: In order to be able to live in society as a person, one must know who one is, that is, have discovered one's real self and, thereby, one's existential relationship with others. In order to make this fundamental self-discovery, one must have a sense of personal existence apart from the veneer of society, that is, a sense of one's existential freedom and responsibility in love. More generally, Merton suggests that a society, particularly as reflected in its educational priorities, that does not aim to provide an environment in which the formation of the whole person will find acceptance and support is clearly alienated from what is true and real.

Merton's view of person in relation to society supports another important conclusion: Education that provides for self-discovery, in enabling one to become a person, enables genuine community to form as well. It is precisely in standing in some sense outside society that the person can form genuine community. The distinctions Merton establishes between individual and person, and collectivity and community, help clarify this seeming inconsistency. In direct correspondence to the distinctions he makes between the true and false selves, Merton often contrasts person and individual in terms of their social counterparts, community and collectivity. "The person," Merton says in *New Seeds of Contemplation*, "must be rescued from the individual," that is, from a life of uprootedness and division, in which identity is determined by the impersonal "mass."[145] According to Merton: "Individualism is nothing but the social atomism that has led to our present inertia, passivism, and spiritual decay. . . . This individualism, primarily an economic concept with a pseudospiritual and moral facade, is in fact mere irresponsibility. It is and has always been not an affirmation of genuine human values but a flight from the obligations from which these values are inseparable. And first of all a flight from the obligation to love."[146] In contrast, "the vocation of the *person* is to construct his own solitude as a *conditio sine qua non* for a valid encounter with other persons, for intelligent cooperation, and for communion in love. From this cooperation and communion

... there grows the structure of a living, fruitful, and genuinely human society."[147] Especially clear from this passage, person and community implicate one another. Just as the growth of the person depends on relationship, the growth of the community depends on the person's capacity for genuine relationship in love. To recall the qualities of the true self, the person relates wholly, capable of communing "in the subjectivity of the one loved." It is relationship in this existential sense that enables community to form. Much more than place, what is common in community so formed is a shared personal identity in love. In keeping with their root meaning (essentially, "common"), communication in such community implies the kind of knowledge-by-identity and participation in the common life of love that Merton associates with the true person. This participation again implies openness, receptivity, responsiveness, and responsibility in dialogue and community activity; that is, a ready willingness to be moved by love rather than individual need or desire.

In comments that he made at a conference aiming to promote open dialogue between Eastern and Western monastic traditions, Merton explains the basis for this view of communication: "And the deepest level of communication is not communication, but communion. It is wordless. It is beyond words, and it is beyond speech, and it is beyond concept. Not that we discover a new unity. We discover an older unity. . . . What we have to recover is our original unity. What we have to be is what we are."[148] Self-discovery—learning to be what we are—ultimately means learning to communicate on this deepest level.

SUMMARY AND PROSPECTS

I have aimed in this chapter to explicate and interpret "self-discovery" as Thomas Merton's idea of the purpose of education. Fulfilling this aim has entailed delving into the Christian contemplative view of life exemplified both in Merton's writing and his living. The meaning of self-discovery has been established in relation to several principal themes in Merton's writing, namely, the "false" and "true" selves, "person," and "community." A host of concepts have been introduced to help develop these themes, including, "ground of being," "unity," "love," "subjective identification," "life," "freedom," and "relationship." Essentially, self-discovery has been viewed, not as an indication of something particular to be found, but as an existential realization which implies a consciousness and orientation of one's whole being in love. Self-discovery, in its existential quality, is at once made and lived.

Merton emphasizes that self-discovery means becoming no more than who one is, albeit who one is in the eyes of God, not in the eyes of the "ego" or "false" self or society at large. This implies first and foremost the free, whole, and indivisible person who Merton refers to as "the very self who finds."[149] Second, it implies personal recognition of individual freedom, dignity, and responsibility. Finally, it implies a deepening interior growth in which the individual person humbly becomes more open to love. To recall from Chapter 2 what Merton expresses simply to friends in a letter: "Our real journey in life is interior: it is a matter of growth, deepening, and of an even greater surrender to the creative action of love and grace in our hearts."[150]

Providing for self-discovery as the purpose of education clearly means, then, understanding and *providing* for an understanding of individual freedom, dignity, responsibility, and personal wholeness. It implies as well discerning and responding to the presence of love in oneself and others. The metaphors "awake" and "attentiveness" help to vivify this aspect of self-discovery.

The "deepening" quality of growth that Merton describes suggests its dialectical nature. Self-discovery, at the same time that it means "a fantastic awakening to the truth and transcendent value of one's *ordinary self*," can be described as a dialectical process in which existential awareness of self and other in "the unity of love" is opened and reopened.[151] Through self-discovery, one moves from being an individual living in an impersonal mass to being a person capable of creating and living in community. This movement is made possible because of the capability of the person to identify wholly with others in love, or, put in another way, to *commune* "in the subjectivity of the one loved."[152]

Self-discovery has a particular ontological basis, indicated in part by the experience of wholeness and unity it implies. As an expression of the capacity of the person to identify subjectively with others in love and to see things in their own unique identity, it implies, as well, a particular epistemology—involving "knowledge-by-identity," or knowledge by and through love (wisdom). A discipline of attentiveness can help prepare one to experience this deeply personal knowledge. In this respect, self-discovery stands in marked contrast to conceptions of educational purpose which stress exclusively cognitive attainments, individual achievement, or the accumulation of static knowledge.

Considered from its particular ontological and epistemological perspective, self-discovery as the purpose of education implicitly suggests the means for its own fulfillment. Education which aims to provide for self-discovery must strive, in other words, to exemplify self-discovery in all its manifestations. To educate for self-discovery—whether in the context of "school" or the broader life of the community—one must educate in some sense from "within" it, that is, educate as a person. Inasmuch as self-discovery means finding out who, in existential terms, one already is, such education seems indeed possible.

To be "educated," in Mertonian terms, ultimately means having developed an "active and creative awareness of love."[153] It is for this awareness that education conceived in the name of self-discovery should aim. This is Merton's central message: In order to become who we are, in order to live fully and wholly as human persons, we must recognize first of all the reality of our inner selves, our capacity for love, and our true existence in the unity of love. This entails growing in a wisdom accessible only through and realizable only as love. One who personifies the purpose of education as self-discovery has learned that to live and love are the same thing.

Specifically, what might education viewed from the Mertonian perspective of "self-discovery" developed here involve? I would suggest orienting discussion initiated by this question to the following related questions or topics:

• The subject of self-discovery, the true self, is the whole person. What are some of the fundamental areas in and through which the growth of the whole person can be fostered?

• What might be basic characteristics of a person-oriented or personalized approach to education, particularly as reflected in teaching?

• Given Merton's assertion that all learning should dispose one for "self-discovery," how might we insure that the nature of what is learned, and, moreover, that the quality of the learning experience itself, helps foster this disposition?

• The nature of "seeing" so as to apprehend things in their own reality, that is, as they are, respecting their unique identity; the nature of similar faculties of the whole person, such as listening, hearing, and speaking.

• The possible application of disciplines associated with the spiritual life, such as openness and attentiveness, to learning and personal growth, and to such activities as listening, speaking, and writing important in traditional education and in our personal lives.

• The distinction between knowledge which is experienced or apprehended and knowledge gained through reason and analysis.

• Merton's understanding of wisdom in terms of truth and love ("Logos"), and his belief that wisdom is manifest in persons and nature: What, in fact, might "sapiential" teaching entail?

• Creating an environment which gives credence to interior life and subjectivity and which reflects characteristics of the true self. Merton suggests that such an environment "favors the secret and spontaneous development of the inner self."[154] Such an atmosphere also suggests the importance of distinguishing personal growth and formation from individual achievement.

• The prospect of fostering genuine dialogue, in accordance with self-discovery; that is, dialogue which respects the personhood of participants and in which listening, responding, and awakening response are seen in terms of becoming attentive to the movement of love, of truth, of Christ in oneself and in one's community. In this respect, the principles associated with the nonviolent philosophy of Gandhi and Christianity can be very instructive.

• Basic characteristics of Merton's own teaching and understanding of teaching.

• Recognizing the implications of one's existential identification with others through community service and responsibility, in dialogue, and for personal vocation.

In consideration of these topics, subsequent chapters are entitled, "Seeing, Hearing, and Speaking," "Voice and Truth," "Communication, Dialogue, and Communion." Each of these chapters presents an area of personal growth in and through which the formation of the whole person can be fostered. These areas are developed in accordance with Thomas Merton's example and Christian contemplative philosophy. The chapter called "Teaching and the Education of the Whole Person" extends this discussion into the realm of teaching.

Notes

1. Merton, "Learning to Live," in *Love and Living*, p. 10.
2. Ibid., p. 3.
3. Ibid., p. 9.
4. Ibid., p. 7.
5. Ibid.
6. Thomas Merton, *No Man Is an Island* (New York: Harcourt Brace Jovanovich, 1955), p. xv. Merton's introduction to *No Man Is an Island* clearly demonstrates the paradoxical nature of self-discovery.
7. Ibid., p. xvi.
8. Quoted by Merton in *No Man*, p. xv.
9. Ibid., p. xxi.
10. Ibid., pp. xxi-xxii; see also Merton, "The Power and Meaning of Love," *Disputed Questions*, p. 111; on "unity" in a more general sense, see especially Merton, *The Behavior of Titans* (New York: New Directions, 1961), pp. 78-79, 82, and Merton, *New Seeds of Contemplation*, p. 56.

11. Merton, *Disputed Questions*, pp. 119, 207.

12. Daggy, ed., *Introductions*, p. 92 (Merton's introduction to the Japanese edition of his book *Thoughts in Solitude*).

13. Merton, *No Man*, p. xv.

14. Thomas Merton, "The Inner Experience: Prospects and Conclusions (VIII)," *Cistercian Studies*, 19:4 (1984), p. 343; Merton's concern for language "as the medium which unites or divides" also noted by Mott, *The Seven Mountains of Thomas Merton*, p. 381; cf., Merton, *Thoughts in Solitude* (New York: Farrar, Straus & Giroux, 1956), p. 86.

15. Merton, "The Inner Experience (VIII)," p. 345.

16. Merton, "Learning to Live," in *Love and Living*, p. 4.

17. Ibid.

18. Merton, "The Inner Experience (VIII)," p. 345.

19. Merton, *New Seeds*, p. 47.

20. Merton, *Thoughts*, p. 84; *No Man*, p. xvii; *The Behavior of Titans*, pp. 81-82.

21. Thomas Merton, *The New Man* (New York: Farrar, Straus & Giroux, 1961), p. 114.

22. William Shannon, "Thomas Merton and the Discovery of the Real Self," in *The Message of Thomas Merton*, ed. Brother Patrick Hart (Kalamazoo, Mich.: Cistercian Publications, 1981), p. 193.

23. See especially *New Seeds of Contemplation*, *Faith and Violence*, *Zen and the Birds of Appetite*, and "The Inner Experience."

24. Mott, *The Seven Mountains of Thomas Merton*, p. 453. Mott quotes from what are until 1993 Merton's "Restricted Journals" (the passage is from Merton's entry of June 4, 1966); Mott attributes Merton's reflection in part to his response to his love for a nurse from Louisville whom he met during this time.

25. Merton, "The Climate of Mercy," in *Love and Living*, p. 186; also Merton, *Zen and the Birds of Appetite* (New York: New Directions, 1968), p. 22.

26. Thomas Merton, "A Note on *The Psychological Causes of War*," in *Faith and Violence* (Notre Dame, Ind.: University of Notre Dame Press, 1968), pp. 112-113.

27. Merton, *No Man*, p. 221.

28. Merton, "A Note on *The Psychological Causes of War*," in *Faith and Violence*, pp. 111-113.

29. Thomas Merton, "Rain and the Rhinoceros," in *Raids on the Unspeakable* (New York: New Directions, 1966), p. 18.

30. Merton, "The Climate of Mercy," in *Love and Living*, p. 186.

31. Ibid. Although establishing a broad comparative perspective is well beyond the scope of this work, it is significant to note that Merton's description of the psychological aspects of the false self corre-

sponds to similar accounts by other well-known spiritual writers. Of these, the most notable twentieth-century figure is perhaps Martin Buber, the Jewish mystical philosopher whose work was familiar to Merton. Buber states in *I and Thou* that the capacity of an "I" to enter into a direct and genuine relationship with another (a "you") depends on that "I" giving up the "false drive for self-affirmation;" Martin Buber, *I and Thou* (New York: Charles Scribners Sons, 1970), p. 126. One might also consider comparatively *The Cloud of Unknowing*, whose anonymous fourteenth-century author advises that one "must lose the radical self-centered awareness of [one's] own being if [one] will reach the heights of contemplation in this life." *The Cloud of Unknowing* (New York: Image Books, 1973), p. 102.

32. Merton, *The New Man*, p. 101.

33. Ibid., pp. 101-102.

34. A perspective suggested by Merton especially in *The New Man*, pp. 103-104, *Faith and Violence*, pp. 112-113, and "The Inner Experience: Notes on Contemplation (I)," *Cistercian Studies* 18:2 (1983), pp. 3-4.

35. Merton, "Blessed Are the Meek," in *Faith and Violence*, p. 23.

36. Merton to Abdul Aziz, November 17, 1960, in *The Hidden Ground of Love: The Letters of Thomas Merton on Religious Experience and Social Concerns*, ed. William Shannon (New York: Farrar, Straus & Giroux, 1985), p. 45.

37. Merton, "Rebirth and the New Man in Christianity," in *Love and Living*, p. 181.

38. Merton, "The Contemplative Life in the Modern World," in *Faith and Violence*, p. 219.

39. Ibid., pp. 219-220.

40. Merton, "The Inner Experience (I)," p. 3.

41. Merton, "The Contemplative Life in the Modern World," in *Faith and Violence*, pp. 220, 224.

42. Merton, "Time and the Liturgy," *Seasons of Celebration* (New York: Farrar, Straus & Giroux, 1965), pp. 45-60.

43. Merton, "The Inner Experience (I)," p. 4.

44. Merton, "Time and the Liturgy," in *Seasons of Celebration*, pp. 50, 53.

45. Ibid., p. 47.

46. Ibid., p. 51; see also Merton's commentary on time in the context of a discussion of William Faulkner's *The Sound and the Fury*, in *The Literary Essays of Thomas Merton*, ed. Brother Patrick Hart (New York: New Directions, 1981), pp. 499-500, and in *Opening the Bible* (Collegeville, Minn.: Liturgical Press, 1970), pp. 52-59.

47. Merton, "Rain and the Rhinoceros," in *Raids*, p. 18.

48. Merton, "Time and the Liturgy," in *Seasons of Celebration*, p. 45.

49. Merton, "A Note on *The Psychological Causes of War*," in *Faith and Violence*, p. 113.

50. Merton, "'Godless Christianity'?" in *Faith and Violence*, pp. 274-275, 277-278.

51. Ibid., p. 275.

52. Thomas Merton, *Day of a Stranger* (Salt Lake City: Gibbs M. Smith, 1981), p. 31.

53. Suggested in a general way by Mott, *The Seven Mountains of Thomas Merton*, p. 366.

54. Merton, *New Seeds*, p. 279.

55. See Merton, "The Inner Experience (I)," p. 3.

56. Merton, *No Man*, pp. 118, 123.

57. See Merton, *New Seeds*, p. 283; *Zen*, pp. 39, 78.

58. Merton, *The New Man*, pp. 11-13; "Learning to Live," in *Love and Living*, pp. 7-8.

59. Merton, *Zen*, p. 22.

60. Ibid., pp. 25-26.

61. Merton, "The Inner Experience (I)," pp. 5-6.

62. Merton, "Learning to Live," in *Love and Living*, p. 9.

63. Merton, *The New Man*, p. 169.

64. Merton, *New Seeds*, p. 283; *Zen*, p. 25.

65. Merton, *Zen*, p. 25.

66. A point made by Merton in a letter to Erich Fromm; see Shannon, ed., *The Hidden Ground of Love*, p. 314.

67. Merton, *No Man*, p. 225; *Zen*, p. 75.

68. Merton, *Zen*, p. 26.

69. Merton, *Disputed Questions*, pp. 124, 207; *Zen*, p. 75.

70. Merton, *Disputed Questions*, p. 111.

71. Merton, "Learning to Live," in *Love and Living*, p. 9.

72. Merton, "The Inner Experience: Society and the Inner Self (II)," *Cistercian Studies* 18:2 (1983), pp. 121-122.

73. Merton, *The New Man*, pp. 125-126.

74. Thomas Merton, *Life and Holiness* (New York: Image Books, 1963), p. 50; also germane, Merton, *The New Man*, p. 126.

75. Merton, *Zen*, p. 30.

76. Merton, *No Man*, p. 225; "The Inner Experience (II)," p. 124.

77. Merton's essay, "The Power and Meaning of Love," in *Disputed Questions*, pp. 97-126, is especially illustrative.

78. Merton, "The Inner Experience (II)," pp. 121-122; also, Merton, *New Seeds*, p. 29; *Zen*, p. 50.

79. Merton, "The Power and Meaning of Love," in *Disputed Questions*, p. 103.

80. Merton, "The Inner Experience (II)," p. 123.

81. Merton, "The Power and Meaning of Love," in *Disputed Questions*, p. 103; cf., Mott, *The Seven Mountains of Thomas Merton*, p. 344.

82. Merton, "The Power and Meaning of Love," in *Disputed Questions*, p. 126; *Zen*, p. 24; *The New Man*, p. 19.

83. Merton, "The Inner Experience (II)," p. 122.

84. Mott, *The Seven Mountains of Thomas Merton*, pp. 289-291; Mott describes Merton's intellectual and personal involvement with psychoanalysis, including his sad encounter with a psychiatrist named Gregory Zilboorg.

85. Merton, *No Man*, p. xv. "Final Integration: Toward a 'Monastic Therapy,' " in *Contemplation in a World of Action*, (New York: Doubleday, 1971), p. 211; "A Note on *The Psychological Causes of War*," in *Faith and Violence*, pp. 111-112; see also, "Monastic Experience and East-West Dialogue," Appendix IV, *Asian Journal*, p. 310.

86. Merton, "Final Integration," in *Contemplation in a World of Action*, p. 207.

87. Merton, "Learning to Live," in *Love and Living*, p. 9.

88. Merton, "Final Integration," in *Contemplation in a World of Action*, p. 211.

89. Merton, "The Inner Experience (II)," p. 123.

90. Merton to Erich Fromm, October 2, 1954, in Shannon, ed., *The Hidden Ground of Love*, p. 309.

91. Merton, "Final Integration," in *Contemplation in a World of Action*, pp. 205-217.

92. Ibid., p. 211.

93. Ibid.

94. Merton, *No Man*, p. xv.

95. Merton, "Final Integration," in *Contemplation in a World of Action*, p. 211.

96. Merton, *New Seeds*, p. 51.

97. Merton, *No Man*, p. xv; echoed in "Love and Need," in *Love and Living*, p. 31.

98. Merton, "The Inner Experience (II)," p. 123.

99. Merton, "Learning to Live," in *Love and Living*, pp. 7-8.

100. Merton, *Disputed Questions*, pp. ix, x.

101. Merton, "Rain and the Rhinoceros," in *Raids*, p. 16.

102. Merton, *Disputed Questions*, p. x.

103. Merton, *The Way of Chuang Tzu* (New York: New Directions, 1965), p. 17; see also Conference Tape # 265B ("Growing Up Beyond Social World"), February 18, 1968, Thomas Merton Studies Center, Bellarmine College, Louisville, Kentucky.

104. Merton, *Disputed Questions*, p. xi; *New Seeds*, p. 55.

105. Merton, *Conjectures*, pp. 156-157.

106. Ibid., p. 158.

107. Merton, "Rain and the Rhinoceros," in *Raids*, p. 15.

108. Merton, *Conjectures*, p. 158; "Learning to Live," in *Love and Living*, p. 9.

109. Merton, "Blessed Are the Meek," in *Faith and Violence*, pp. 27-28.

110. Merton, "Blessed Are the Meek," in *Faith and Violence*, pp. 14-29; "Gandhi and the One-Eyed Giant," in Merton, ed., *Gandhi on Non-Violence* (New York: New Directions, 1964), pp. 1-20.

111. Merton, "Blessed Are the Meek," in *Faith and Violence*, p. 27.

112. Ibid., p. 28.

113. Ibid., p. 18; see also Merton, "Gandhi and the One-Eyed Giant," in *Gandhi*, p. 19.

114. Merton, "Blessed Are the Meek," in *Faith and Violence*, p. 15.

115. Merton, *No Man*, p. 219.

116. Ibid., p. 225.

117. Ibid., p. 230.

118. Merton, "Time and the Liturgy," in *Seasons of Celebration*, p. 59.

119. Ibid., p. 57. See also, Merton, "Time and Unburdening and the Recollection of the Lamb: The Easter Service in Faulkner's *The Sound and the Fury*," in Hart, ed. *Literary Essays*, pp. 498-514, passim; Merton, *Opening the Bible*, pp. 52-59.

120. Merton, "Time and the Liturgy," in *Seasons of Celebration*, p. 48; see also Merton, *Vow of Conversation*, pp. 32, 116.

121. Merton, *Thoughts*, p. 95.

122. Merton, *The Sign of Jonas*, p. 319.

123. For example: Merton, *The Behavior of Titans*, p. 89; *New Seeds*, pp. 295-297; *Clement of Alexandria: Selections from the Protreptikos* (New York: New Directions, 1962), p. 10.

124. Merton, "Rain and the Rhinoceros," in *Raids*, p. 15.

125. Merton, *The Behavior of Titans*, p. 79; *New Seeds*, p. 296.

126. Merton, *New Seeds*, p. 297.

127. Bhikkhu Khantipalo, "On Mindfulness," in Merton, *Asian Journal*, p. 297. Thich Nhat Hanh, Vietnamese Buddhist monk and friends with Merton, has written similarly that "mindfulness" refers "to keeping one's consciousness alive to the present reality," Thich Nhat Hanh, *The Miracle of Mindfulness* (Boston: Beacon, 1976), p. 11; cf., Buber, *I and Thou*, p. 126: "The one thing needful" to "go forth" from the "It-world," according to Buber, is "the total acceptance of the present."

128. Bhikkhu Khantipalo, "On Mindfulness," in *Asian Journal*, p. 298.

129. Simone Weil, *Waiting for God* (New York: G. P. Putnam's Sons, 1951), pp. 105-116.

130. Ibid., pp. 111-112.

131. Ibid., p. 112.

132. Thomas Merton, *Spiritual Direction and Meditation* (Collegeville, Minn.: Liturgical Press, 1960), p. 53.

133. Merton, *Vow of Conversation*, pp. 110-111.

134. As an additional starting point, see Parker Palmer, *To Know As We Are Known / A Spirituality of Education* (New York: Harper & Row, 1983). Palmer's concept of "obedience" (in its etymological sense of "to listen") would provide a broader basis for clarifying the concept and possible role of attentiveness in the formation of the whole person.

135. Daggy, ed., *Introductions*, p. 92; Merton, "Love and Solitude," in *Love and Living*, p. 16.

136. Merton, "The Power and Meaning of Love," in *Disputed Questions*, p. 123.

137. Ibid., p. 99.

138. Merton, *Thoughts*, pp. 93-94.

139. Merton, *The Way of Chuang Tzu*, p. 17.

140. Merton, "The Inner Experience (II)," p. 124.

141. Suggested especially by Merton's discussion in *Disputed Questions*, pp. x, xi, and *The New Man*, p. 91.

142. Merton, *Thoughts*, p. 13.

143. Merton, "Christianity and Totalitarianism," in *Disputed Questions*, p. 148.

144. Merton, *Thoughts*, p. 13.

145. Merton, *New Seeds*, pp. 38, 48; *Disputed Questions*, pp. x, xi.

146. Merton, *Disputed Questions*, p. x.

147. Ibid., p. xi; see also "The Christian in World Crisis," in *Seeds of Destruction* (New York: Farrar, Straus & Giroux, 1964), pp. 163-164.

148. Merton, "Thomas Merton's View of Monasticism," Appendix III, *Asian Journal*, p. 308.

149. Merton, "Learning to Live," in *Love and Living*, p. 4.

150. Merton, "September 1968 Circular Letter to Friends," Appendix I, in *Asian Journal*, p. 296.

151. Merton, "A Note on *The Psychological Causes of War*," in *Faith and Violence*, p. 114.

152. Merton, "The Power and Meaning of Love," in *Disputed Questions*, p. 103.

153. Merton, *Zen*, p. 69.

154. Merton, "The Inner Experience (I)," p. 6.

4

Seeing, Hearing, and Speaking

As Merton moved in his interior journey from separation to more concrete, compassionate identification with the people of his world he was compelled to view and eventually to respond to the world in fundamentally new ways. Paradoxically, solitude and silence nurtured a more mature social vision and a voice bold, challenging, critical, honest, and unrelenting in its effort to confront illusion and bear witness to truth.

Merton's vision and voice were disciplined by faculties of seeing, hearing, and speaking grounded in his interior experience of life. Thus they were intimately linked to his Christian contemplative viewpoint. These faculties reflect a basic capacity for understanding and knowing the world rooted in personal (subjective) experience. Their development in concert with the effort to learn about self and the world will clearly be vital to the growth of the whole person. What is the origin and nature of these faculties? How do they serve as a form of spiritual discipline essential to the formation of the whole person?

SEEING

In order to understand Merton's social vision (not in the sense of *a* vision, but in the basic ways he looked at and understood society) one must try to understand what "seeing" in general meant for Merton, including what it meant in terms of personal relationship to the natural world. Metaphors of sight and, conversely, of blindness and illusion figure prominently in both Merton's spiritual and social writing. They provide an important indication of his own understanding and practice of the discipline of seeing; consequently, they suggest the significance of this discipline to "the formation of the whole person."

"The first step in the interior life," Merton writes in *No Man Is an Island*, ". . . [is] unlearning our wrong ways of seeing, tasting, feeling, and so forth and [acquiring] a few of the right ones."[1] The "right" way of seeing involves, in part, developing "the ability to respond to reality, to see the value and beauty in ordinary things."[2] In keeping with Merton's contemplative perspective, this way of seeing emphasizes apprehending things as much as possible as they are and not as one may suppose or want them to be. "We must not only use [things] but value their use, and appreciate them justly for what they really are," he says in *The New Man*.[3] Characteristic of "seeing," then, as it pertains to external reality is a simple appreciation, if not a celebration, of the ordinary things of life.

There is also a level of seeing on which one not only apprehends a visible thing as it is but becomes conscious of a deeper significance preserved in its "very being and nature." In his introduction to Merton's *Selected Poems*, Mark Van Doren, one of Merton's literature teachers at Columbia University and a life-long friend, cites a letter in which Merton speaks of this form of insight: " 'The earliest [church] fathers knew that all things, as such, are symbolic by their very being and nature, and all talk of something beyond themselves.' "[4] Thus, in Merton's poetry, according to Van Doren, "all the senses work together to one end, the letting of things declare themselves."[5] Certainly the ability of poets such as Gerard Manley Hopkins and Rainer Maria Rilke to evoke the meaning intrinsic to the "very being and nature of things" similarly contributed to Merton's admiration of their work.

Merton tried in the early 1960s to broaden his poetic vision with the aid of a camera, using film to capture "not the imitation but the image" of an object which portrays "a new and different reality."[6] John Howard Griffin, Merton's mentor in this effort, explains that Merton's "passion [for photography] was simply for another means for expressing his vision: the challenge to capture on film something of the solitude and silence and essences that preoccupied him."[7] At about this same time, Merton began to create "calligraphies" or "graffiti," which were "signs" that stood as free, momentary intimations or intuitions of a deeper reality not found "on the level of conception or concept." These signs "came to life when they did . . . as expressions of unique and unconscious harmonies appropriate to their own moment though not confined to it."[8] Merton's "signs" point to the "something beyond themselves" talked of by things, and the "new and different reality" he enjoyed trying to capture in photographic images. Merton's beautiful prose poem, *Hagia Sophia*, which he composed in 1961, expresses perhaps most eloquently his intimation of what this "new and different reality" is: "There is in all visible things an invisible fecundity, a dimmed light, a meek namelessness, a hidden wholeness. This mysterious Unity and Integrity is Wisdom/the Mother of all/Natura naturans."[9]

To see, then, implies both apprehending things as they are and cherishing in their simple, unique "being and nature" (seeing that they are—"being"—and seeing them as they are—"nature"—is itself a revelation) an intimation of wholeness and unity, something which is not "seen" in any ordinary sense. Indeed, as Merton explains in his letter to Mark Van Doren, "Their [things'] meaning is not something we impose upon them, but a mystery we can discover in them, if we have the eyes to look with."[10] Seeing involves a relaxation of one's own natural effort to supply meaning, a willingness to experience with our whole selves on an existential level, an acceptance of and openness to mystery. This acceptance does not, however, imply passivity. Quite otherwise, as Mark Van Doren points out, "The right eyes for the purpose are keen and honest, and there had better be some humor in them."[11] Seeing, as developed here, can rightly be viewed as a discipline requiring practice and sensitivity. As Merton once wrote, "I find that as a monk I have a full-time job simply trying to be clear sighted for two minutes a day."[12] In *New Seeds of Contemplation* he wonders "if there are twenty men alive today who see things as they really are. That would mean that there were twenty men who were free."[13]

Any difficulty in Merton's efforts to gain clearer vision was compounded by the prevalence of illusion and falsity he perceived in both himself and his society. "To say we are born in sin," Merton wrote in *The Secular Journal*, "is to say we are born in illusion and blindness."[14] Blindness, on a personal level is the effect of our inherent self-centeredness and selfishness.[15] We are inhibited from seeing reality more as it is because we are immersed in a ceaseless pursuit of our own desires to the point where "desire itself becomes our chief satisfaction."[16] However well-intentioned, this self-entangled pursuit, the contrivance of the false self, sadly becomes "our only substitute for joy."[17] Desire can promote blindness even when what is desired is the ideal of clear vision or greater integrity of vision and life. Merton noted from his hermitage in 1965 that "what I find most in my whole life is illusion, wanting to be something of which I have formed a concept."[18] For Merton, the challenge of day-to-day attentiveness in the life of solitude helped preclude an illusory existence.

To dispel our self-inflicted blindness, we need to recognize first of all the futility of our search for self-fulfillment in the pursuit of things. This in fact is one level of "seeing" as it pertains to ourselves.[19] By working to disengage ourselves from that pursuit, we begin to actualize our capacity to see things as they are, to see "their value and beauty." This form of detachment is thus not a matter of renouncing self or things, or, least of all, life. Rather it is in all humility a full recognition of and rejoicing in that which is.[20] We begin to see dimly through our own prejudice and cupidity to a reality and beauty independent of our own will and desire. We begin to see and build a more authentic relationship with the world. "We are called to become fully real," Merton wrote in his Japanese introduction to *The New Man*, "by attaining to a reality beyond the limitations of selfishness."[21]

On a deeper, personal level, seeing involves the realization that our own dignity and beauty rests in who we *are*, in our "being" (ultimately our being in God), and not intrinsically in our willed action, which is so often harnessed by our desire for visible achievement.[22] Furthermore, it means recognizing that the same "hidden wholeness" reflected uniquely in each thing is also inherent in us; or, more deeply, that it is in the "hidden wholeness" of God that we, with things, inhere. To "see" in this sense means trying *not* to see ourselves first and foremost in terms of tangible things that can be measured. It is difficult, Merton would say, to see anything beyond ourselves when we hold ourselves forth as the one measure of what is real and true.[23] As he explains in *No Man Is an Island*,

I do not need to *see* myself, I merely need to *be* myself. I must think and act like a living being, but I must not plunge my whole self into what I think and do, or seek always to find myself in the work I have done. . . .

The reason why men are so anxious to see themselves, instead of being content to be themselves, is that they do not really believe in their own existence. . . . They must struggle to escape their true being and verify a false existence by constantly viewing what they themselves do. . . . They are hoping for some sign that they have become the god they hope to become by means of their own frantic activity—invulnerable, all powerful, infinitely wise, unbearably beautiful, unable to die![24]

The path to true wholeness and being is dramatically otherwise. It is precisely in recognizing and accepting our basic human vulnerability, in confronting the fact of our nakedness and pow-erlessness before death, in realizing our need for love and, ultimately, our dependency (our contingency) on God, that we are most free, most open, and most likely to see, if not to hear and speak, with greater clarity.[25]

It is clear that "seeing," as it pertains both to the apprehen-sion of external reality and the corresponding understanding of illusion in oneself, is the sensate expression of humility. "To grow up means in fact to become humble, to throw away the illusion that I am the center of everything," Merton writes in *The New Man.*[26] He might add that clarity of vision and humility grow interdependently. One cannot "see" external reality without to some extent relinquishing the self-centered illusion of power and invulnerability. One cannot likewise grow in hum-ble awareness of one's tenacious hold on illusion without to some extent being able to "see" the "value and beauty" of things, and recognize in their unique, independent character a manifestation of the "hidden wholeness" also intrinsic to us. Similarly, one cannot fully identify with other persons in the "unity of love" (Merton's understanding of solitude) without genuine humility and "seeing." Simply put, we see more clearly as we are less blinded by illusion, that is, as we are more genu-inely humble. The two qualities grow in a complementary, dia-lectical way.

"Humility," Merton explains, "consists in being precisely the person you actually are before God."[27] "The person you actual-

ly are" means the person stripped of selfishness and illusion to a
bare existential level, the whole person detached from "works"
and "reputation," from, indeed, one's self-image.[28] Yet it would
be a mistake to interpret such humility as a total self-effacement
or self-renunciation. In the language of Merton's contemplative
spirituality, humility implies a centering of one's life on God, at
the same time that it suggests an opening of one's life more
wholly to people (greater identification) and the world in love.[29]
Merton's sympathetic description of the " 'comic' humility" of
Chuang Tzu, a Chinese philosopher of about the third century
B.C., is illustrative. Chuang Tzu's humility is "rooted in the true
nature of things . . . full of life and awareness, responding with
boundless vitality and joy to all living beings."[30] True humility
clearly does not imply self-constraint, but freedom: "In humility
is the greatest freedom."[31]

Annie Dillard, author of *Pilgrim at Tinker Creek,* suggests how
the experience of seeing in particular ways can enrich, if not
transform, one's experience of self and the world.[32] Dillard
moves through several levels in her discussion of "seeing," beginning with the simple challenge of taking greater notice of the
fecundity of life around her at Tinker Creek. The prospect of
noticing more, of trying to become more aware, becomes to
some extent an act of humility: "But if you cultivate a healthy
poverty and simplicity, so that finding a penny will literally
make your day, then, since the world is in fact planted in pennies, you have with your poverty bought a lifetime of days. It is
that simple. What you see is what you get."[33] If, on the other
hand, one is "so malnourished and fatigued" so as to neither
acknowledge nor notice the plenitude of "pennies cast broadside from a generous hand," then one suffers an impoverish-
ment of seeing— "so I cut myself off, not only from the total
picture, but from the various forms of happiness."[34]

As an example of seeing that is at once more primal, more
innocent, and in effect more childlike (not affected by predis-
posing concepts and values), Dillard cites the experiences of
"newly sighted" people upon seeing the world: "Many newly
sighted people . . . teach us how dull is our own vision. . . . A
little girl visits a garden. She is greatly astonished . . . stands
speechless in front of [a] tree, which she only names on taking
hold of it, and then as 'the tree with the lights in it.' "[35] Dillard
ponders what it would be like to see "color-patches" like the

little girl did, "the world unraveled from reason, Eden before Adam gave names." "The scales would drop from my eyes," she asserts.[36] It is this kind of innocent contact with reality, devoid of any meaning save the pristine and intimate experience of wonder, that Merton would exult in as well. Of "cave man's art," for example, he says, "[It] was before all else a celebration of [direct awareness] and of the *wholeness* of his communion with nature and with life. . . . Today with a myriad of instruments we can explore things we never imagined. But we no longer *see* directly what is right in front of us."[37]

Dillard mentions "another kind of seeing that involves a letting go."[38] "Letting go" evokes strongly a humility of vision, of seeing in such a way that one does not impose meaning on a scene, but, in keeping with Merton's respect for the "very being and nature" of things, waits for and receives it. Dillard likens this seeing to the action of a camera: "When I walk without a camera, my own shutter opens and the moment's light prints on my own silver gut. When I see this . . . way I am above all an unscrupulous observer."[39] "The secret of seeing," Dillard concludes lyrically, "is to sail on solar wind. Hone and spread your spirit till you yourself are a sail, whetted, translucent, broadside to the merest puff."[40] Here she implies a level of consciousness on which what is seen is not *made* present (not the product of analysis and, perforce, reason) but allowed to *be* present. Seeing thus becomes an experience of the whole person and suggests that celebration of wholeness ("hidden wholeness") and connectedness to natural reality to which Merton was so attuned.

Briefly recounted here, Dillard's description and experience of different levels of seeing affirm and to some extent illustrate the basic quality of seeing vital to the growth of the whole person as understood by Merton. If one is only able to see according to prescription, preconception, or even the prejudice of names and categories, if, in another words, one is unable to notice, be surprised, moved, and taken by the natural world, then blindness and illusion will undermine one's personal capacity for free and whole response to life.

HEARING

Hearing, no less than seeing, stems from openness and humility. And, just as seeing involves noticing beyond ourselves, hear-

ing requires a discipline of listening unencumbered by preconceived notions about what one might hear. As in seeing, one's
listening is attuned to natural reality, at the same time that it
occurs on a level of consciousness deeper than that defined by
concept or idea. Merton suggests these dimensions of hearing in
a characteristically paradoxical style when he writes in "Love
and Solitude": "No writing on the solitary, meditative dimensions of life can say anything that has not already been said
better by the wind in the pine trees. These pages seek nothing
more than to echo the silence and the peace that is 'heard' when
the rain wanders freely among the hills and forests. . . . The
Hearer is No-Hearer."[41] One cannot actually "hear" on a level
of consciousness on which there is no actual sound, but only a
deeper resonance of that sound. When one hears in such a way
that the real, natural world is made more present, and "hears"
as well "the deeper silence," one begins to understand true
solitude, in which one "is attuned to all the Hearing of the
world."[42] As Merton explains, this means "living on a certain
level of consciousness" which comprehends, without words, "the
undivided unity of love."[43] There are no "words" on this level of
consciousness because " 'words' are not love, for they are many
and Love is One."[44] But "that One Word [Love] is heard only in
the silence and solitude of the empty heart, the selfless, undivided heart, the heart that is at peace, detached, free, without
care."[45]

"Seeing" and "hearing," in Merton's contemplative view, both
imply a level of meaning experienced beyond, yet, to a certain
"level of consciousness," accessible through sense. This level of
understanding, therefore, is not so much sensory or reasoned as
experiential, experiential on an existential level, and thus reflecting the integrity of our own fundamental and subjective
wholeness. Merton expresses this level of meaning variously as
"hidden wholeness," "Wisdom," the "One Word" (Love), and
"the hidden ground of love." It is realized more in the realm of
interior silence than in rationality and analysis. It is as basic as
life itself. For Merton, it reflects the active and loving presence
of God, as Creator, in all life. When one becomes better able to
see and hear, one is more attuned to this fundamental reality of
life. As Merton came to realize more and more in the solitary
life, one acts more freely as one becomes more attentive to deep
inner response, and one's life becomes more fruitful:

The great joy of the solitary life is not found simply in the beauty and peace of nature . . . or even in the peace of one's own heart. It resides in the awakening and the attuning of the inmost heart to the voice of God—to the inexplicable, quiet definite inner certitude of one's call to obey Him, to hear Him . . . in the realization that this is the whole reason for one's existence.

This listening and this obedience make one's existence fruitful and give fruitfulness to all one's other acts.

The voice of God is not clearly heard at every moment; part [of what is needed] is *attention*. . . . What this means, therefore, is not only attention to inner grace but to external reality and to one's self as a completely integrated part of that reality. Hence, this implies also a forgetfulness of one's self as totally apart from outer objects, standing back from outer objects; it demands an integration of one's own life in the stream of natural and human and cultural life of the moment. When we understand how little we listen . . . we realize how important this inner work is.[46]

Merton emphasizes that the capacities to "see" and "hear" wholly are integral to human living and thus suggests that actualizing them will be essential to the growth of the whole person. His viewpoint can only be understood from the perspective that these are not acquired capacities but innate faculties indicative of the inherent, loving relationship of God and humanity. Hence, Merton points out in "Notes on Art and Worship" that "the world of the spirit is not something quite apart from the world of the senses. The two are in fact inseparable and form a single whole."[47] Similarly, he suggests that "seeing" and "hearing" are exemplified more in the child's innocent grasp of natural reality than in the notions of how and what one should see and hear held forth by society.[48] This implies a capacity for wonder, a capacity to behold. Seeing and hearing in this innocent sense need to be rediscovered, cultivated, renewed, and to some extent freed from the distracting formulas of society.

In order to appreciate the possibility of seeing and hearing according to this interpretation of Merton's view, one must understand them in their simple and natural childlike quality. In terms of the natural world, one is not searching for some preconceptualized, extraordinary essence apart from the thing itself; Merton does not construct a duality of object and essence.

Rather, the "essence" is synonymous with the thing itself. As mentioned earlier, it is the particular, intrinsic quality of the natural thing, its "very being and nature" (expressive of whole-ness, grounded in love) to which Merton refers.

To say that seeing and hearing are inborn, natural faculties is not to suggest that they are easily developed. The "formation of the whole person," insofar as it implies the development of these faculties, also involves a process of deepening humility, and, as noted in the previous chapter, means developing a sense of personal identity more fundamental than the illusions of who one is or should be often foisted by society upon its members.[49] Merton devoted much of his adult life to realizing his unselfish, independent spiritual identity in concert with the effort to see and listen more freely and clearly. His poetry, photography, graphic "signs," and journal writing testify especially to this effort. He similarly recognized in art, music, and other forms of creative expression the potential to uniquely reflect and evoke the deeper levels of human experience and reality.[50] Merton's manifest desire to bring himself and others into more intimate, authentic, and whole contact with reality was his expression of the life of "invisible fecundity. . . [and] hidden wholeness . . . at once my own being, my own nature, and the Gift of My Cre-ator's Thought and Art within me."[51]

SPEAKING

Like seeing and hearing, the capacity to speak—more specifi-cally, the unique ability to form words—both expresses and emerges from the innate capacity to apprehend "the very na-ture and being" of things and persons, and the "hidden whole-ness" that they intimate. Merton addresses this subject directly in his chapter entitled "Free Speech" in *The New Man*.[52]

Merton couches his discussion of "free speech" in the story of Adam in Genesis, noting that God brought the newly formed animals to Adam to see what *he* would name them. The cre-ative, naming capability thus given to Adam signified Adam's unique, participatory role in God's work of creation (" 'for that which the man called each of them would be its name.' "— Genesis 2:19). Hence, as represented by Adam, "man not only learns how to look at things and see them for what they are, but acquires means of conveying his idea of them to others. Here begins the dialogue with other men."[53] On this level, dialogue is creative, celebratory, reverent: "Words, names, and signs . . . will flower into many kinds of creative intellectual activity. They will become, first of all, poems which will express man's inexpressible intuitions of hidden reality of created things. They will become philosophy and science. . . . Finally words will become *sacred* signs. They will acquire the power to set apart certain elements of creation and make them holy."[54] Viewed from this perspective, words assume a particular dignity, a reverential quality, and an evocative power; we have a "wonderful capacity," Merton says, to "make things intelligible and full of light in ourselves."[55] But this is true only insofar as our words emerge from the honest depths of silence in ourselves—"Even if we never talk to anyone . . . the mental word . . . stands in the depths of our intelligence to bear witness to reality and to worship God."[56] He says further, in *Thoughts in Solitude*, "[We] cannot understand the true value of silence unless [we have] a real respect for the validity of language, for the reality which is expressible in language is found, face to face and without medium, in silence."[57]

Just as in a photograph, as Merton suggests, one can create an image expressive of reality, in a word one can create a symbol of one's intuition of real. Recognizing and developing this capability is "of the greatest importance," according to Merton. "The language and thought of [the person]," he writes, "need to rise above the level of distinct concepts which, though they may give us accurate information, fall short of the existential mystery of things they represent."[58] Indeed, Merton notes that for Adam, in the pristine moments of primal speech, "the primary function of language was to bear witness to the hidden meaning of things rather than to 'talk about' them."[59] This capability implies a particular attentiveness to language analagous to the disciplines of seeing and listening as they have thus far been described. Our capacity to form words can be said to correlate with our capacities to see and hear. In order to speak a word more in accord with what we see and hear as whole persons, that represents our whole selves, we will need to attend to our inmost experience in silence; we will need to allow the word to form in silence. On the other hand, to use language indifferently on a regular basis or to "focus on the symbol rather than on what it symbolizes" is to close off one's interior response and thus to diminish to some extent who one is as a whole person and one's corresponding interior growth.[60] Merton put it in another way in a conference at Gethsemani: "In a certain way, my word is *myself;* when I form an interior word about a situation, that word is me in relation to that situation. . . . Speech is something that absolutely has to be controlled. . . . If all our [exterior] communication is on a low level . . . all the things that go along on the surface of life . . . all our interior activity becomes shallow. . . . I stop thinking."[61]

"Speaking," for Merton, like "seeing" and "hearing," clearly has the quality of a discipline. Words are to be deeply respected as symbols both of the human power to create and the reality of creation and, more, as expressions of our whole selves. Thus they emerge not simply from our own thought and analysis but from silence, the silence in which our relationship to a "situation," and more deeply to reality, can be known. One can readily infer that our care with words—more precisely, our care in attending to the origin and formation of our words—will bear significantly on our perception of and relationship to reality and will accord with our care in seeing and listening. Moreover, inasmuch as they can convey essential meaning to others, our words can have a significant bearing on their growth as well; like art or music, they can prove transformative. Finally, as discussed in the next chapter ("Voice and Truth"), our capacity to speak, in conjunction with our capacities to see and hear, will together form the quality of our "voice." Education aimed at "the formation of the whole person" clearly must address the importance of how one forms the words to express what one "sees" and "hears."

"RAIN AND THE RHINOCEROS"

As noted in the previous chapter, the power of society to collectively create and perpetuate illusion was one of Merton's most unsettling concerns. Illusion fabricated on a social scale insinuated itself on a personal scale, thus enervating the capacities to see, hear, and speak. "We are a generation of [people] who have eyes and see not, ears and hear not, because we have let ourselves be so completely and abjectly conditioned by words, slogans, and official pronouncements," he wrote in *Disputed Questions.*[62] Merton was alert for any form of manipulation, whether ideological, psychological, institutional, or political, which falsely created, distorted, or preyed upon human needs and thus precipitated futile efforts at need satisfaction. He felt strongly that the sensory stimulation inundating society through the media, particularly in the form of advertisements, diluted the possibility of clearer vision and hearing.[63] Essentially, these elements of the social ethos inhibited the formation of the whole person.

Perhaps nowhere in his writing does Merton present his concern with socially fabricated illusions vis-à-vis the formation of the whole person more effectively, or more instructively, than in "Rain and the Rhinoceros."[64] In this essay, he addresses in particular the socially consecrated credo that views time, things, and people in terms of "use." "Rhinoceros," an image Merton borrows from a Eugene Ionesco play, connotes the blind, charging impulse of " 'modern man' " to make both time and things functional or " 'useful.' "[65] "Rain," on the other hand, in the presence of one who can be silent and listen, is a free and pure festival. But, Merton warns, this hardly makes it invulnerable to manipulation at human hands.

> Let me say this before rain becomes a utility that they can plan and distribute for money. By "they" I mean the people who cannot understand that rain is a festival, who do not appreciate its gratuity, who think that what has no price has no value, that what cannot be sold is not real, so that the only way to make something *actual* is to place it on the market. The time will come when they will sell you even your rain. At the moment it is still free, and I am in it. I celebrate its gratuity and its meaninglessness.

> Think of it: all that speech pouring down, selling nothing, judging nobody, drenching the thick mulch of dead leaves, soaking the trees, filling the gullies and crannies of the wood with water, washing out the places where men have stripped the hillside! What a thing it is to sit absolutely alone, in the forest, at night, cherished by this wonderful, unintelligible, perfectly innocent speech . . . the talk that rain makes by itself all over the ridges. . . .

> As long as it talks, I am going to listen.[66]

In the midst of Merton's mythopoetic vision of the rain, society's utilitarian values come crashing in: "They [the city people] have constructed a world outside the world, against the world, a world of mechanical fictions which condemn nature and seek only to use it up, thus preventing it from renewing itself and man."[67]

Merton's contrast of "rain" (nature) and "the rhinoceros" (blind, human impulse) is, and is undoubtedly meant to be, jarring. Yet Merton's purpose is clearly not to evoke a response which simplistically equates nature with "innocence" and society with corruption.[68] Nor is it simply to awaken a consciousness that will tend toward a greater appreciation of nature and condemnation of its callous treatment at society's hands. His principal focus is rather on the development of the whole person in the context of modern society—on, more specifically, those values which alienate the person from natural reality and consequently from the capacity for a deeper interior response and sense of self ("the invulnerable inner reality . . . which we can only *be*").[69]

Merton celebrates the "gratuity and meaninglessness" of the rain. Modern society, in contrast, celebrates and finds meaning only in what is "useful," in the artificial, usually monetary, terms which it defines. Usefulness, Merton implies, becomes the measure of reality both for the collectivity and the individual. Thus, it is blinding and deafening. It prevents people from truly seeing or hearing the unguarded speech of the rain or understanding it as an example of authentic speech. It forces them to consider only what is "useful," in the world, in time, or in themselves, as real. They cannot appreciate what is free as real ("rain") because they have been pressed into blind conformity with the "collective obsession." They cannot therefore discover their own freedom in their deeper identity as whole persons.

For Merton, submission to the "collective obsession" is clearly an imprisonment of the whole person. In order to recognize and liberate oneself from the prison of "necessity," one must stand still, confront one's essential aloneness (in solitude), and learn to see and listen. If unable to listen to the rain, one fails to experience its basic power of renewal. Whereas the "rhinoceros" rushes blindly ahead, the whole person, it can be said, stays behind to listen; to live, in other words, more in accord with and more attuned to our intimate and ever-renewing relation with reality.

Merton draws a momentary parallel to Henry David Thoreau in his text. Certainly a comparison is provocative and informative. Both the tone and substance of "Rain and the Rhinoceros" resonate harmoniously with aspects of Thoreau's *Walden*. Both Merton and Thoreau write in physical solitude from their cabins in the woods. Thoreau decried the encroachment of human technology, principally in the form of the railroad, on nature. Merton wondered in a more general way about "a world that has, well, progressed" (his most powerful image is a "SAC plane"—"loaded with strong medicine"—which flies through the serenity of the Gethsemani night).[70] Thoreau, "self-appointed inspector of snow storms and rain storms," fills his pages with images that reflect what he has seen or heard of the reality around him or that illustrate a particular quality of seeing or hearing. ("We must learn to reawaken and keep ourselves awake . . . by an infinite expectation of the dawn."[71]) Merton's listening to the rain is comparably alive and awake, open and reverent. Also like Thoreau, Merton confronts conformity masked as freedom. And, just as Thoreau sensed a "quiet desperation" in the lives of his contemporaries, Merton marked the hidden despair in the restless charge of "the rhinoceros."[72]

There are levels of significant difference in the work of Merton and Thoreau which can be briefly mentioned within the narrow boundaries of comparison delineated here. One involves the question of personal identity and reality. Unlike Thoreau, for example, Merton discusses identity and nature in terms of the concrete experience of God. Merton's acknowledgement that in such realms as literature, words and symbols can point to if not bring one into a living participation with "an experience of basic and universal human values" balances this point of difference.[73] Merton suggests another level of difference when he wonders whether "Thoreau already guessed that he was part of what he thought he could escape."[74] In contrasting "rain" and "the rhinoceros," Merton was not implying his separation from society. He was, on the other hand, urging separation from the illusions of society, urging us to safeguard our inviolate nature, our capacity for seeing, hearing, and speaking rooted in a reality transcending the contrived world of use and object, possession, manipulation, and unfreedom.

This latter point is important to understanding the theme which unifies "Rain and the Rhinoceros." Merton is not interested in identifying the illusory value of "use" and the creation of false need in society for the self-righteous aim of tearing it down. His primary intent is to show that our lives as whole persons are built on another basis.

Merton frames his central purpose with a question whose answer directly involves the reader: "And where is the power of error?" he asks. "We find it was after all not in the city, but in *ourselves*."[75] With this response, Merton characteristically brings himself and the reader squarely into the focus of discussion. If the reader has developed any anger at a society bent on manipulating the rain, s/he is abruptly asked to respond to it by looking within. In the honest, humbling, vulnerable experience of interior solitude, one's illusions and self-deceptions are stark and clear; and it is in solitude and love that one realizes one's "true capacity for maturity, liberty, and peace."[76]

Merton invokes the wisdom of Philoxenus, a hermit of about the sixth century, A.D.[77] Philoxenus advises us, Merton says, that our growth as whole persons will begin in the aloneness and vulnerability which constitute the basic experience of solitude. In learning to be "alone" (that is, free, unattached to a social definition of self, aware of our "invulnerable inner reality"), our senses will become more awake, our needs simpler and more natural, and our empathy, compassion, and our capacity for identification with others deeper. Merton in this way implies that the renewal of a sense of fundamental value and relationship in society will begin first and foremost in a personal transformation of heart. Meanwhile, he suggests that the "rain," in its glorious gratuity and meaninglessness, will be a source of renewal for us, provided, of course, that we are willing "to listen."

"Rain and the Rhinoceros" is Merton's strong invitation to us to use our senses in a way more in accord with what he perceived as our true freedom. The process of learning to look and see, listen and hear, and to speak, as these capacities have been characterized here, will clearly be integral to "the formation of the whole person." Without the development of these faculties, one hazards an existence based most securely on illusion and therefore only tenuously on freedom, love, and truth.

Notes

1. Merton, *No Man*, p. 33.

2. Ibid. Ten years after publication of *No Man Is an Island*, Merton remarked in his private journal (restricted from public view until 1993, twenty-five years after his death), after a spring rain, on the monk's vocation to bear "witness to the value and goodness of simple things and ways and loving God in it all"; recorded in John Howard Griffin's *Follow the Ecstasy* (Fort Worth, Tex.: Latitudes Press, 1983), p. 33. Griffin was the first of two "authorized" Merton biographers (the other being Michael Mott) to have access to Merton's private journals before 1993 in conducting his research, as prescribed by the Merton Legacy Trust.

3. Merton, *The New Man*, p. 80.

4. Thomas Merton, *Selected Poems* (New York: New Directions, 1959), p. xiii; for additional perspective, see Merton, *New Seeds*, pp. 29-31, and "Notes on Art and Worship," in which he writes, "By artistic and creative genius, man rises above the material elements and outer appearances of things and sees into their inner nature;" quoted in Deba P. Patnaik, ed., *Geography of Holiness* (New York: Pilgrim Press, 1980), p. xiii.

5. Merton, *Selected Poems*, p. xv.

6. Merton, *Conjectures*, p. 149. See also Mott, *The Seven Mountains of Thomas Merton*, p. 344.

7. Griffin, *Follow the Ecstasy*, p. 10.

8. Merton, *Raids*, pp. 180-181.

9. Thomas Merton, *Hagia Sophia*, in *Thomas Merton Reader*, ed., Thomas McDonnell (New York: Image Books, 1974), p. 506.

10. Merton, *Selected Poems*, p. xiii.

11. Ibid.

12. Merton, "Cold War Letters," 1961-1962 (Louisville, Ky.: Bellarmine College, Thomas Merton Studies Center, unpublished), #96, p. 158.

13. Merton, *New Seeds*, p. 203.

14. Merton, *The Secular Journal*, p. 196.

15. Merton, *New Seeds*, p. 43.

16. Merton, "Vision and Illusion," in *Merton Reader*, p. 379.

17. Ibid.

18. Merton, *Vow of Conversation*, p. 140.

19. Cf., Buber, *I and Thou*, p. 126: "What has to be given up is not the I but that false drive for self-affirmation which impels man to flee from the unreliable, unsolid, unlasting, unpredictable, dangerous world of relation into the having of things."

20. See Merton's chapter, "Everything That Is, Is Holy," in *New Seeds*, pp. 21-28.

21. Daggy, ed., *Introductions*, p. 116.

22. See Merton's chapter, "Being and Doing," in *No Man*, pp. 117-130.

23. Again comparison with Martin Buber offers provocative perspective: "This is the activity of the human being who has become whole: It has been called not-doing, for nothing particular, nothing partial is at work in man and thus nothing of him intrudes into the world." Buber, *I and Thou*, p. 125.

24. Merton, *No Man*, pp. 118-119.

25. See, for example, Merton, *Raids*, p. 15, and "Thomas Merton's View of Monasticism," Appendix III, *Asian Journal*, p. 306: "The marginal man accepts the basic irrelevance of the human condition, an irrelevance which is manifested above all by the fact of death. . . . He struggles with the fact of death in himself, trying to seek something deeper than death; because there is something deeper than death, and the office of the monk or marginal person, the meditative person or the poet is to go beyond death even in this life, to go beyond the dichotomy of life and death and to be, therefore, a witness to life."

26. Merton, *The New Man*, p. 103.

27. Merton, *New Seeds*, p. 99.

28. Ibid., pp. 43, 45, 58, 119.

29. Ibid.

30. Merton, *The Way of Chuang Tzu*, p. 27.

31. Merton, *New Seeds*, p. 57.

32. Annie Dillard, *Pilgrim at Tinker Creek* (New York: Bantam Books, 1974).

33. Ibid., p. 16.

34. Ibid., pp. 16-17.

35. Ibid., p. 30.

36. Ibid., p. 32.

37. Merton, *Conjectures*, pp. 307-308.

38. Dillard, *Pilgrim*, p. 33.

39. Ibid.

40. Ibid., p. 35.

41. Merton, "Love and Solitude," in *Love and Living*, p. 14.

42. Ibid., p. 15.

43. Ibid., pp. 15, 17.

44. Ibid., p. 17.

45. Ibid., p. 18.

46. Merton, *Vow of Conversation*, pp. 188-189.

47. Quoted from Merton's "Notes on Art and Worship" by Patnaik in *Geography of Holiness: The Photography of Thomas Merton*, p. xi.

48. Conference Tape 265B, "Growing Up Beyond Social World," February 18, 1968, Thomas Merton Studies Center, Bellarmine College, Louisville, Kentucky.

49. Ibid., see also section on "The True Self" in Chapter 3.

50. See note 4 above, and, for example, "Sacred Art and the Spiritual Life," *Disputed Questions*, pp. 151-164, and " 'Baptism in the Forest': Wisdom and Initiation in William Faulkner," in *The Literary Essays of Thomas Merton*, pp. 92-116.

51. Merton, *Hagia Sophia*, in *Merton Reader*, p. 506.

52. Merton, *The New Man*, pp. 71-98.

53. Ibid., p. 84.

54. Ibid., pp. 84-85.

55. Conference Tape 135B ("Silence and Making Signs: Interior Word Behind Speech"), Thomas Merton Studies Center; see also Merton, *Thoughts*, p. 69.

56. Merton, *The New Man*, p. 88.

57. Merton, *Thoughts*, p. 114.

58. Merton, *The New Man*, p. 85.

59. Ibid., p. 89.

60. Ibid., p. 87. See also Merton, "The Inner Experience (VIII)," p. 343.

61. Conference Tape #135B, "Silence and Making Signs: Interior Word Behind Speech," Thomas Merton Studies Center.

62. Merton, "Sacred Art and the Spiritual Life," in *Disputed Questions*, p. 153.

63. Merton, *No Man*, p. 33, and "War and the Crisis of Language," in *The Nonviolent Alternative*, ed. Gordon Zahn (New York: Farrar, Straus & Giroux, 1971), pp. 234-247.

64. Merton, "Rain and the Rhinoceros," in *Raids*, pp. 9-23.

65. Ibid., p. 21.

66. Ibid., pp. 9-10.

67. Ibid., p. 11.

68. Merton's thinking evolved to this point after many years in the monastery; see Mott, *The Seven Mountains of Thomas Merton*, p. 357.

69. Merton, "Rain and the Rhinoceros," in *Raids*, p. 15.

70. Ibid., p. 14; see also Merton, *Vow of Conversation*, pp. 128-131.

71. Thoreau, *Walden,* pp. 118, 172.

72. Ibid., p. 111.

73. Merton, " 'Baptism in the Forest': Wisdom and Initiation in William Faulkner," in Hart, ed., *Literary Essays,* p. 98.

74. Merton, "Rain and the Rhinoceros," in *Raids,* p. 12.

75. Ibid., p. 19.

76. Ibid., p. 22.

77. Ibid., p. 14.

5

Voice and Truth

THE CHILD'S VOICE

Merton concludes "Letter to an Innocent Bystander," one of his essays collected in *Raids on the Unspeakable*, with an illustrative reference to "The Emperor's New Clothes," a story popularized by Hans Christian Andersen.[1] The tale itself involves an emperor deceived by two swindling tailors into believing that they can weave him a wonderful suit of clothes visible to all but those unfit for their "post" or "hopelessly stupid." The sartorial ruse is well played out; the "suit" is sheer artful fabrication. More striking, however, is the blind complicity of both king and people in the tailors' clever plan. Whether because they do not trust in their own goodness and honesty or fear their own possible exposure and embarrassment (or both), the people are unable to see or acknowledge the actual nakedness of the king parading before them. Only a little child, the "little innocent" in the Andersen version, retains this capability. It is the child's innocent voice ("But he hasn't got anything on!") which keeps the fault of the others "from being criminal," as Merton suggests.[2]

Merton refers to "The Emperor's New Clothes" in particular to draw attention to the quality of innocence represented by the child. The child's innocence is expressed by a wholly honest seeing of what is and a voice sincere, unpretentious, and forthright in declaring that truth. His or her exclamatory remark is utterly spontaneous, thus unmeasured and without ulterior motive.[3]

Merton distinguishes the innocence of the child from a questionable kind of innocence represented by the "bystander"—one of those (including especially intellectuals and monks) who set themselves apart from or over and against society as totally detached observers. Merton implies that self-righteousness, or worse, emptiness and despair, can develop under the guise of such innocent detachment. The posture of "bystander" becomes in effect a pretext for escape and irresponsibility. Merton suggests in this instance the implicit alliance of the bystander with those in society (e.g., those who live in the service of power) with whom s/he claims no allegiance.[4]

Merton does not repudiate the role of bystanders such as himself in society but urges the strengthening of innocence and authenticity in the bystander's voice. He emphasizes first of all that the bystander is inextricably a part of, not apart from society (thus his query with respect to Thoreau in "Rain and the Rhinoceros"); one cannot conscionably retreat or pretend to disappear. At the same time, however, one cannot see or speak clearly as a bystander if immersed wholly in a "program of action" or crusade designed to ameliorate social ills. He suggests instead that the bystander's best and necessary contribution will come from a kind of innocence which doesn't pretend to have a solution, which is bound neither to the politics of power nor the self-satisfaction of isolation. Merton has in mind an innocence akin to that of the child, an innocence which sees and gives voice to truth and reflects a basic trust in life. As he states it:

> The true solutions are not those which we force upon life in accordance with our theories, but which life itself provides for those who dispose themselves to receive the truth. Consequently our task is to dissociate ourselves from all who have theories which promise clear-cut and infallible solutions and to mistrust all such theories, not in a spirit of negativism and defeat, but rather trusting life itself, and nature, and if you will permit me, God above all. For since man has decided to occupy the place of God he has shown himself to be by far the blindest, and cruelest, and pettiest and most ridiculous of all the false gods. We can call ourselves innocent only if we refuse to forget this, and if we also do everything we can to make others realize it.[5]

In order to cultivate above all a trust for life and nature and ultimately "the hidden ground of love," God, the bystander by implication must develop a particular quality of seeing, hearing, and speaking. The practice of these disciplines can itself provide an important witness to life, and this witness can be vocalized in a way which confronts illusion and untruth in society.

Put in a general way, Merton implies that the quality of one's voice in society, one's message, will not depend ultimately on the correctness of what is said as measured against a particular standard, be it theoretical, social, legalistic, or even countercultural or ethical. Rather, it will rest on how well, as called for in a particular situation, one has looked and listened for (disposed oneself "to receive") and then tried to communicate the truth as presented: After all, the child in "The Emperor's New Clothes" is scrupulously honest without intending to be; without, in fact, intending to be anything particular at all (thus "innocent"). One seeks to speak, in other words, a truth understood in one's own wholeness, and which, in endeavoring to see, hear, and speak well, one is wholly disposed to receive. The "innocent" voice will not pretend to know more. Yet in its very innocence it can confront and awaken, if not engage, others' sensibility of truth.

Merton's Personal Voice

In his introduction to *Conjectures of a Guilty Bystander* (written in 1965), Merton makes clear his own effort to ensure a certain quality of "innocence" in his public voice:

> These notes add up to a personal version of the world in the 1960s. . . . They are an implicit dialogue with other minds, a dialogue in which questions are raised. But do not expect to find "my answers." I do not have clear answers to current questions, and, as a matter of fact, I think a man is known better by his questions than by his answers. To make known one's questions is, no doubt, to come out in the open oneself. . . . I question nothing so much as the viability of public and popular answers, including some of those which claim to be most progressive. . . . The total result is a . . . confrontation of twentieth century questions in light of a monastic commitment.[6]

The "innocence" of Merton's "notes" or "conjectures" lies first of all in their nature as questions. Merton steadfastly avoids the pretense of providing answers; least of all does he seek to defend some arbitrary or predetermined position. It is precisely the need for making claims or harboring hidden motives that he wants to eliminate. Thus he attains to a level of honesty and authenticity consistent with his monastic effort to strip away pretense in his personal life.

Merton's "conjectures" represent a "personal" vision developed "in light of a monastic commitment." As he did so often, Merton is careful not to ascribe to himself or to his work anything which would reflect or evoke a particular prejudice. In keeping with his monastic commitment, he aspires to a certain level of humility or "innocence" in his voice, so that, like the child, he can speak from a clearer perspective than that provided by the blinding illusions of society.[7] He aims to establish his "dialogue" with others on insight built from an effort to reduce prejudice (or illusion and blindness) in himself, a dialogue in this sense more truthful; he thus invites a like openness and response. In this respect, Merton's personal example echoes an observation he had made a decade before writing *Conjectures* in *No Man Is an Island*: "A man of sincerity is less interested in defending the truth than in stating it clearly, for he thinks that if the truth be clearly seen it can very well take care of itself."[8] In 1955, however, when *No Man Is an Island* was written, Merton perhaps did not anticipate the extent to which he would personally confront and engage his society in stating the truth.

The quality of authenticity or "innocence" Merton aimed for in *Conjectures*, and represented more archetypally by the child in "The Emperor's New Clothes," constitutes one important characteristic of his "voice" as a monastic "bystander." This and other basic characteristics are reflected in the emergence and conscious development in the 1960s of what can be called his "social" voice, that is, his unprecedented outspoken moral response to questions involving peace and social justice. They are also evident in what and how he spoke in such contexts as monastic renewal. Clarified and elaborated, the attributes of Merton's personal voice will help illustrate the basic quality of voice which can be said to reflect and bear on the formation of the whole person.

If "Letter to an Innocent Bystander" presented Merton's thoughtful appraisal of the precarious role of "bystander" in society and his view of some of the basic characteristics of the "voice" of the bystander, it did not make it any less difficult for him to assume that role. As more and more a vocal "bystander" during the early 1960s, Merton was particularly vulnerable; he was, as Michael Mott puts it, "brought . . . into the realm of public censure."[9] He (as well as the censors of his monastic order!) struggled considerably with both his understanding of what it meant to be in that position and the implications of his faithfulness to it, or more accurately, to the truth that he disposed himself to receive. It was a fruitful struggle, however, because in it Merton began to clarify and exemplify the nature and importance of speaking out.

Merton's effort to clarify his own position as a bystander was often framed in terms of vocational or social questions, and dealt as frequently with the apparent contradictions that arose when these particular frames of reference were applied. Was it possible, for example, to be both a contemplative monk and a social critic? Did the contemplative have a specific role in the "world of action"? And, from the perspective of social activists of the 1960s who came to consider Merton an ally, was the "bystander" a legitimate position at all? Indeed, was the bystander, by definition, a model of irresponsibility in the face of compelling social need? What, implicitly, determined quality of voice? Could one in fact speak efficaciously? If so, to what end?

In confronting these questions, Merton suffered, doubted, meditated, persevered. In the first of his "Cold War Letters," written during the nascent period of his outspokenness sometime in the spring of 1961, his sense of vulnerability and conviction are both apparent: "Prayer of course remains my chief means [of responding to the need for peace], but [there is] also an obligation on my part to speak out insofar as I am able, and to speak as clearly, as forthrightly, and as uncompromisingly as I can. A lot of people are not going to like this and it may mean my head, so do please pray for me in a very special way . . . because I cannot in conscience willingly betray the truth or let it be betrayed."[10] Commenting on both this passage and Merton's concurrent journal reflections, Michael Mott concludes that Merton at this time had "doubts about his physical courage," was "fearful of disapproval" and "unsure of himself." In Mott's estimation, Merton "took a certain pleasure in smashing his early public image," yet "felt a real sense of dread in the image he was assuming."[11]

In spite of substantial insecurity and fear and the burdensome question of whether it was appropriate for a monk to speak out, Merton clearly intended to stand firm in faithfulness to "the truth." He subsequently initiated a stream of articles addressing social concerns and attesting to his belief in a way of being different from those he saw dominating his world. His alarm at the destructive threat to life posed by nuclear weapons and the moral insensibility he felt they grotesquely mirrored galvanized his early efforts. By 1962, a lone yet strong monastic voice, he had written and published substantially on these interrelated topics. His pioneering social commentary included, notably, *Original Child Bomb* (the Japanese designation for the Hiroshima bomb), "The Root of War Is Fear" (included in *New Seeds of Contemplation*), and articles such as "The Shelter Ethic" and "Nuclear War and Christian Responsibility."[12]

For Merton, the question of whether it was right or appropriate to speak out as a monk was clearly subordinate to a greater necessity and responsibility. In his personal correspondence, particularly with such members of the peace movement as Dorothy Day, Daniel Berrigan, and James Forest, he aired his fears even as he honed his viewpoint. In his public and monastic writings he unabashedly proclaimed his position. Merton's social voice can in this respect be considered closely linked to his voice of monastic renewal, that is, to his call for a renewed understanding of the contemplative life, indeed, for a renewed appreciation for life itself. Considered together, these expressions of Merton's voice point to the more fundamental origin and characteristics of voice in general.

Whether in spite of or because of his concern about the consequences of his social writing, Merton left little room for friends to misunderstand his determination to propound his views. For example, he explains his "Cold War Letters," his ongoing series of epistolary essays circulated broadly to friends during 1961 and 1962, as "nothing more than the expression of loyal but unpopular opinion, of democratic opposition to what seem to be irresponsible trends. Without such voices raised in opposition to grim policies and majority compulsions, democracy would be without meaning."[13] Merton makes clear that he would not hesitate to speak "forthrightly" and "uncompromisingly" as the situation demanded. Yet Merton's perspective was not as readily accepted within his monastic order. As he felt increasingly compelled to speak, his voice was challenged by a corresponding reluctance on the part of his monastic superiors to provide such opportunity.

Merton did not begin his period of greatest response to social questions without exciting some of the controversy he had uneasily anticipated. Involvement with the world's concerns, even in the form of writing, was problematical from the prevailing monastic point of view; Merton's own evolving sense of identification with the people of the world, however, would lead him to carefully question this perspective throughout the sixties. Meanwhile, as his writing on peace proliferated, Merton's abbot general (a leader in the Trappist monastic order) became more adamant in upholding the traditional monastic stance.

After reminding him of the difference between an order that teaches and one that prays, Dom Gabriel Sortais wrote to Merton in May of 1962: "Please understand that I am not asking you to remain indifferent to the fate of the world. But I believe you have the power to influence the world by your prayers and by your life withdrawn into God far more than by your writings. . . . I ask that you give up your intention of publishing the book [on issues of peace in the nuclear age] you have just finished, and abstain from now on from writing on the subject of atomic warfare, preparation for it, etc."[14] Merton's response to Dom Gabriel's censure was in part relief; he was leery himself of overzealousness in carrying out a cause.[15] Clearly, however, prayer could not suffice for him as the sole means of expressing his interest in "the fate of the world." The seeds of moral protest (latent in his experience of relationship to others in solitude) had found a sturdy soil in the critical issue of nuclear war. Indeed, in one of his early letters to Dorothy Day, written eight months before Dom Gabriel's stricture, Merton confided:

[Censorship] is a very great problem to me. Because I feel obligated to take very seriously what is going on, and to say whatever my conscience seems to dictate, provided of course that it is not contrary to the faith and to the teaching authority of the Church. Obedience is a most essential thing in any Christian and above all in a monk, but I sometimes wonder if, being in a situation where

obedience would completely silence a person on some important
moral issue on which others are also keeping silence—a critical issue
like nuclear war—then I would be inclined to wonder if it were not
God's will to ask to change my situation. . . . I don't feel I can in
conscience . . . go on writing about things like meditation, though
that has its point. . . . I think I have to face the big issues, the life-
and-death issues; and this is what everyone is afraid of.[16]

Merton did not ask to change his "situation," but he continued
to write, and moreover to circulate mimeographed copies of the
proscribed material to friends. Since strictly speaking not "published," this mimeographed distribution became Merton's way
of disseminating his new and provocative ideas.[17] Merton's
"Cold War Letters," whose circulation numbered in the hun-
dreds, including friends inclined to pass their copies along,
served this same purpose.[18]

Particularly in light of the rejuvenation of Catholic Church
perspectives inspired by the Vatican II Council in the early
1960s, and Merton's own considerable efforts on behalf of monastic renewal, censorship of Merton's social writing was gradually relaxed. What is important to note here, however, is the fact
of Merton's continued writing activity on behalf of peace in the
face of censure and his additional effort to establish an alternative avenue for disseminating his ideas. In continuing to write
and distribute his work, Merton was not acting subversively
according to a loose, but reasonable, interpretation of Trappist
monastic guidelines, and particularly his vow of obedience.[19]
But this effort in itself can still be considered an important
measure of his persistence and determination in speaking out.
It is natural in this respect to ask what prompted Merton, and
what, relatedly, distinguished and characterized his "voice."
The effort to answer these questions—in other words, to clarify
further the motivation for and basic quality of Merton's voice—
will strengthen the basis for discussing the quality of voice implied by "the formation of the whole person."

"By the spring of 1962," in Michael Mott's judgment, "Merton's public image had been radically changed."[20] In spite of his
initial fears and ambivalence, and the prospect of likely censure,
Merton was making his views and voice of moral protest well
known. To some, the tone and tenor of protest seemed in dis-

turbing contrast to these same dimensions of Merton's popular spiritual writing. Yet what might seem different in style or focus reflected not so much a radically new Merton as perhaps a change from the image of Merton others had formed. Merton's "social voice"—though unquestionably harsh at times and sometimes overdrawn—was not out of step with his growth toward greater identification with others "by hiddenness and compassion," nor did it reflect a major discontinuity with his sense of vocational commitment or the spiritual insight represented by his meditative writing. It might be said instead that Merton was living now more deeply, boldly, and freely—though hardly more assumingly—in light of his maturing interior life and spiritual conviction.

Merton's introduction to the Japanese edition of *The Seven Storey Mountain*, written in late summer 1963, suggests the spiritual connection between his growing and compassionate identification with others in his world and his voice of protest. He builds from his explanation that "by being in the monastery I take my true part in all the struggles and sufferings of the world":

> To adopt a life that is essentially nonassertive, nonviolent, a life of humility and peace is in itself a statement of one's position. But each one in such a life can, by the personal modality of his decision, give his whole life a special orientation. It is my intention to make my entire life a rejection of, a protest against the crimes and injustices of war and political tyranny which threaten to destroy the whole race of man and the world with him. . . . I am saying NO to all the concentration camps, the aerial bombardments, the staged political trials, the judicial murders, the racial injustices, the economic tyrannies, and the whole socio-economic apparatus which seems geared for nothing but global destruction in spite of all its fair words in favor of peace. I make monastic silence a protest against the lies of politicians, propagandists, and agitators . . . The faith in which I believe is also invoked by many who believe in war, believe in racial injustices, believe in self-righteous and lying forms of tyranny. My life must, then, be a protest against these also.[21]

This passage demonstrates the characteristic integrity of Merton's message and example. His contemplative life and social voice of protest, as exemplified in and by his statement, cohere;

they are both grounded in his deeper experience of an inherent relationship with others than that which the physical boundaries between monastery and "world" might imply. It is clearly because he took part "in all the struggles and sufferings of the world" that Merton did not make his life a protest against *people*, but rather against "crimes," "injustices," "tyrannies," and the "socio-economic apparatus." Hence his protest is also at once a witness to "monastic silence." This is not silence in the ordinary sense of "quiet," in which there is no real listening or hearing. By "monastic silence" Merton means the silence beyond thought in which one can become attuned to a deeper level of reality and relationship, the place of self-discovery in which one can begin to recognize oneself whole in relationship to others in the love of God. The significance of Merton's voice of social protest for "the formation of the whole person" lies first of all in its origin in silence, not in the content of the protest itself, as important as that is. As Merton's remarks from the Japanese introduction to *The Seven Storey Mountain* indicate, authentic personal voice and silence are not opposed or independent of each other but in fact constitute complementary aspects of a single whole. Merton makes an analogous observation regarding music in *No Man Is an Island* which illustrates this point more eloquently: "Music is pleasing not only because of the sound but because of the silence that is in it; without the alternation of sound and silence, there would be no rhythm."[22] Merton's understanding of dialogue in the 1960s would incorporate his deep sense of the rhythm of sound (words, speech) and silence.[23]

Whether implicitly or explicitly, Merton deferred consistently to the primal level of reality and relationship experienced in silence in explaining his voice of protest. For example, miffed at the censorship of his writings on peace, Merton complains in a Cold War Letter to peace activist Jim Forest, "The monk is the one supposedly attuned to the inner spiritual dimension of things. . . . [Yet] he must be an eye that sees nothing except what is carefully selected for him to see. An ear that hears nothing except what it is advantageous for the managers for him to hear. We know what Christ said about such eyes and ears."[24] In another instance, less than a year after he wrote his introduction to the Japanese edition to *The Seven Storey Mountain*,

Merton the bystander asserted, "The monastic community is deeply implicated . . . in the economic, political, and social structure of the contemporary world."[25] This thought prefaced Merton's *Seeds of Destruction*, a series of powerful commentaries on race relations, social justice, and peace written in light of his contemplative perspective. Merton added that "to forget or to ignore this does not absolve the monk from responsibility for participation in events in which his very silence and 'not knowing' may constitute a form of complicity."[26] Merton goes on to explain the origin of this responsibility in the traditional terms of his vocation: "To have a vow of poverty seems to me illusory if I do not in some way identify myself with the cause of people who are denied their rights and forced, for the most part, to live in abject misery. To have a vow of obedience seems to me to be absurd if it does not imply a deep concern for the most fundamental of all expressions of God's will: the love of His truth and our neighbor."[27] Merton sounds here the depth of his traditional monastic vocation. Speaking out is not perceived as a sign of infidelity to vows but, in a spirit of renewal, and particularly in the context of pressing moral and social issues, a deeper response to them. "True obedience," Merton explains to James Forest, is "synonymous with love."[28] Again, Merton's voice of protest and voice of monastic renewal have a common origin in his deeper sense of identification with others and deeper experience of love. And love compels a particular discipline, sincerity, and authenticity in voice.

A significant measure of his effort to ensure the authenticity of his own voice, Merton formulated and sounded his perspective on the role of the contemplative in speaking out in society through his trusted correspondence with persons such as Dorothy Day and Daniel Berrigan. Merton's letter of June 25, 1963, to Daniel Berrigan is noteworthy in this respect. To Berrigan, a prominent figure in the peace and nonviolent resistance movements beginning in the early 1960s, Merton articulated his pivotal questions: "What is the contemplative life if one doesn't listen to God in it? What is the contemplative life if one becomes oblivious to the rights of men and the truth of God in the world and in His Church?"[29]

To those who would question whether a monk could have a social voice, Merton would clearly reply that it was precisely because of his vocation, more specifically his contemplative life as a monk, that the development of his own voice was not surprising. One could expect stronger identification with "the struggles and sufferings of the world" as an outgrowth of contemplative experience. The voice of social concern that emerged genuinely from contemplative experience was therefore not a contradiction and did not in any sense diminish the call to a contemplative life, its importance, or its necessity. If anything, the fact that a contemplative might be called, if not compelled in certain instances (e.g., involving race or peace), to bring his or her unique perspective on reality and life to bear on particular problems of what was also their world made it all the more important that one strive to be a good contemplative.[30] Merton even suggested that "a certain openness to the world and a genuine participation in its anguish would normally help to safeguard the sincerity of a commitment to contemplation."[31] This perspective would be important for Merton in the 1960s not only in addressing the question of monastic renewal but in distinguishing the call to protest from the call to action.

What exactly would the monk—specifically the contemplative—speak *for*? Merton's introduction to the Japanese edition of *The Seven Storey Mountain* gives ample evidence of what he was protesting *against* and suggests what prompted his speaking out. It points to the origin of voice in silence and grounds the voice of moral protest in love and the reality of deeper relatedness and identification with others. Less vigorously stated, but no less significant for understanding his motivation and purpose, is what Merton was affirming by his example and voice. "If I say NO to all these secular forces," he explains, "I also say YES to all that is good in the world and in man. I say YES to all that is beautiful in nature, and in order that this may be the yes of a freedom and not of subjection I must refuse to possess any thing in the world as purely my own. I say YES to all the men and women who are my brothers and sisters in the world, but for this yes to be an assent of freedom and not of subjection I must live so that no one of them may seem to belong to me and that I may not belong to any of them."[32] In a more general sense, Merton affirmed realizations essential to his growth as a whole person in the contemplative life: the inherent value and beauty of natural reality; his fundamental identity with others as persons; and the understanding of both natural reality and persons in their inviolate freedom; that is, their freedom from manipulation, use, or any false identity imposed on them by himself or his society, their freedom rooted in their independent identity in what Merton apprehended as the hidden ground of being or love.

One cannot keep in perspective what Merton was generally protesting against in the 1960s without understanding what he was affirming. Similarly, one cannot fully understand his action in speaking out from the silence of Gethsemani without appreciating that his voice and example were a testimony to what he experienced as real in solitude and what his contemplative life allowed him to see and hear.

What motivated and molded Merton's voice of protest, therefore, was also what he sought to affirm. His voice emerged from silence and testified to what in silence was revealed as real, to life. In silence resounded an innocence and authenticity beyond his own predilection, his own thought, his own prejudice and that of his society; thus silence attuned him to understanding on a level of existential reality and nurtured authenticity in his own voice. To speak authentically from silence, therefore, required a vigilant openness and disinterest, in effect the same attentive process of learning to see, hear, speak, and discern inherent to the formation of the whole person. Merton would not only ask himself to engage in this process but also the others who would protest with him in the 1960s, or who struggled in the effort to convert protest into constructive action.

Merton's voice, then, reflected a basic unity of message and example, of voice and life, of belief and experience. This integrity by itself, however, did not give Merton's voice its strength, its honesty, and what has been recognized as its uncanny prophetic quality.[33] What has to be likewise emphasized is his effort to give voice to something greater than himself, yet fully accessible to his understanding (to his "seeing" and "hearing"), thus reflected in himself as well—the reality of "hidden wholeness," the basic truth of life itself as a manifestation of God's love.

To cast discussion in general terms, Merton was speaking against illusion and falsity and, indeed, against all in himself, others, and his society which he had come to realize in his interior journey as unreal or untrue or which diverted one from seeing, hearing, or speaking the truth. Conversely, he was speaking for and attesting to what was real, to life itself.

Merton maintained strongly that the appreciation of life in its actuality, if not the capacity for such appreciation, was lost in the maze of myth, false and fabricated need, jargon, ideology, propaganda, and violently projected fears that constituted what was essentially an ersatz reality in society. Already noted, Merton spoke on behalf of life in "Letter to an Innocent Bystander": "The true solutions are not those which we force upon life in accordance with our theories but those which life itself provides for those who dispose themselves to receive the truth."[34] In *Thoughts in Solitude* (1956), one of his highly regarded spiritual and meditative works, he had written, "The solution of the problem of life is life itself."[35] And in the mythical, dream-like "Atlas and the Fatman," he speaks directly for the wonderful singularity of life: "Every plant that stands in the light of the sun is a saint and an outlaw. Every tree that brings forth blossoms without the command of man is powerful in the sight of God. . . . Every blade of grass is an angel singing in a shower of glory. These are worlds of themselves. No man can use or destroy them. . . . You fool, it is life that makes you dance; have you forgotten?"[36]

The theme of life had endeared Boris Pasternak's *Dr. Zhivago* to Merton in the late 1950s; that is, life, irrepressible, overflowing the bounds of both "recorded history" and "nation."[37] The main characters in *Zhivago*, Yurii and Lara, stand themselves as a silent, transcendent testimony to life in the face of the social and ideological upheaval besetting post-Czarist Russia in the early twentieth century. Pasternak provides a voice for their symbolic, yet fully sentient experience: "How good to be alive and to love life! Oh, the ever-present longing to thank life, thank existence itself, to thank them as one being to another being."[38] It was precisely Pasternak's faith in the existential and spiritual dimensions of life (represented especially by Lara[39]), undaunted by the events of twentieth-century Russia, that made *Zhivago* such a powerful statement to the modern world for Merton.[40] It was such existential confidence that he sought to rekindle through his own work.

"Life," for Merton, then, did not simply denote nature, still less mere biological fact. Life was a matter of "being," being as

celebrated by Yurii and Lara in *Dr. Zhivago,* whose source is
God. Thus life itself has a meaning transcending human design,
yet intimated in the fact of humans "being"; as another Pasternak character, Nikolai, suggests, "Communion between mortals
is immortal. . . . The whole of life is symbolic because it is
meaningful."[41] In invoking "life," Merton clearly asks that we
attend to a meaning that is both greater than and as evident as
ourselves.

Though not alluding specifically to nature when speaking of
life, Merton is suggesting that our identity as whole persons will
never be fully realized unless a deeper connection between the
life of nature and our own lives is taken into account by the
modern worldview; that disinterest and respect, rather than
indifference and domination, must mold our relationship with
nature.

In affirming life, Merton does not by inference disavow modern society; he does not suggest that modern society is incapable of developing an ethos which opens its members to life and
which is thus conducive to the formation of the whole person.[42]
Merton gained perspective on this question through his study of
archaic and primitive societies, suggesting in general that many
of their assumptions regarding reality and life could bear his
society's honest reflection.

In discussing, for example, the ancient Zapotecan culture of
Monte Albán, an erstwhile city of the Oaxacan Valley of Mexi-
co, Merton writes, "It is above all salutary for us to realize that
[peace, tranquility, and security] were possible only on terms
quite other than those which we take for granted as normal. In
other words, it is important that we fit the two thousand war-
less years of Monte Albán into our worldview. It may help to
tone down a little of our aggressive, self-complacent superiority
and puncture some of our more disastrous myths."[43] The
"terms" to which Merton refers involve, fundamentally, an understanding of reality and identity in contradistinction to the
predominant assumptions of modern Western society. The Za-
potecans of Monte Albán, on the one hand, realized their identity as part of, not apart from, their natural and cultural world,
in which the gods, too, made their home. The "sacred" and the
"worldly" were thus united; one knew where one " 'be-
longed.' "[44] The conception of identity commonly held in West-

ern society, on the other hand, rests on a basic separation of subject and reality; it is "subjective and psychological . . . centered on the empirical ego regarded as distinct and separate from the rest of reality."[45]

Merton implies that Western society reveres the presumed distance between subject and reality, in contrast to the "primitive" society of Monte Albán which perceived person and reality as inextricably interconnected. He does not as a result urge the adoption of the "primitive" cultural point of view as an idyllic counterpart to our own. But he does suggest that the person who achieves identity over and against or apart from natural reality (as compared to identification with reality) may be inhibited from developing a more intimate and whole relationship with the world. If untempered in Merton's view, the subjective (implying self-centered) conception of identity fostered by the dualism of self and reality in Western society will tend to condone myths which support overly aggressive, dominating, and exploitive attitudes.

In highlighting the difference between Zapotecan and Western conceptions of identity, Merton clearly aims to call into question his own society's self-assurance and monolithic ethnocentrism; to put it simply, its belief that what it thought was right was indeed right and, moreover, best for itself, if not for the rest of the world.[46] His overall intent was to initiate a process of honest self-reflection in his society that would open it to living more attuned to reality, thus more whole.

Merton's interest in cultural anthropology was not simply a means for him to establish intelligent perspective on his society's assumptions of life and reality. It also served the more basic purpose of deepening his apprehension and appreciation of the varied dimensions of elemental human experience.

Merton's unfinished and most ambitious poetic effort, *The Geography of Lograire,* perhaps best expresses his celebration of the elemental and personal in life as reflected in the diversity of human culture. In a letter to his friend Wilbur Ferry, he described the poem as "my summa of offbeat anthropology."[47] In its content the poem presents an anthropological mosaic, interweaving a variety of authentic cultural images and perspectives unbounded by time, yet associated by general geographical direction (north, south, east, and west). Merton emphasizes this aspect of the poem in his introductory note and suggests that the overall creative effect is a vision of the elemental and the personal in human experience. "The poet," he explains, "more and more . . . realizes that this world is at once his and everybody's. It cannot be purely private any more than it can be purely public. It cannot be fully communicated. It grows out of a common participation which is nevertheless recorded in authentically personal images."[48] Merton's poem can be viewed as the creative fruit of his love of life and person as they are uniquely expressed in human culture, and not simply as they are viewed through a single cultural lens.[49] It thus stands as a creative affirmation of life, of the multifaceted wholeness of human existence unencumbered by ethnocentric perspective.

Merton's anthropological interests and cross-cultural perspectives help demonstrate the extent of his effort to affirm and open others to life in its wholeness. Most important is his underlying message that the wholeness of life and the life of the whole person are coextensive, in unison, reflective of each other; they are not, therefore, in the prevalent mode of Western society, determined solely by the subject identified over and against reality. By implication, the development of voice in the formation of the whole person will involve attuning to and learning to articulate what is in concert with life in its wholeness, and to open, in this way, life to others and others to life. The voice of the whole person will thus strive to distinguish, and resist speaking from or for, the illusions and harmful myths of society. Merton's abiding hope was that members of his society might learn to speak with such a "whole" voice; his concern, that certain aspects of the technology, beliefs, and practices of his society might enervate this mature human capacity.

Merton's dismay at modern society's preoccupation with technology, especially evident in *Conjectures of a Guilty Bystander*, stems from his concern that it will militate against the formation of the whole person, thus eroding the capacities to apprehend life in its wholeness and to appreciate the other, too, as a whole person. He feared the allure of technology, its appeal to the need for power and control which feeds on the ethnocentric mentality, and thus its potential to become both means and end in modern society, itself the substitute for reality. Merton maintained at one point that "the central problem of the modern world is the complete emancipation and autonomy of the technological mind at a time when unlimited possibilities lie open to it. . . . Technology has its own ethics of expediency. What *can* be done efficiently *must* be done in the most efficient way."[50] In spite of this view, Merton did not categorically renounce technology; he later observed in a more temperate tone that technology can "elevate and improve man's life" but only on the condition "that it remains subservient to his *real* interests; that it respects his true being; that it remembers that the origin and goal of all being is in God."[51] Characteristically, the pivotal question for Merton was whether technology would help or hinder the person's whole growth and the capacity to apprehend life genuinely, in its wholeness. More specifically, he was concerned with whether the experimental discoveries of science would be exploited by technology and business or integrated in the deeper perspective represented by the "qualitative, experiential, and personal values developed in monastic life."[52]

Merton was acutely aware of any aspect of society which placed the person in some way in a position of servility. He cautioned that even "ethics" could serve this ignominious purpose—by superimposing a formula or legalism on the person. "Ethics," he asserted, "is not simply a code of rules by which one learns to play social games"; rather, it must aim at "the complete formation of the human person."[53] He elaborates by suggesting that ethics ultimately "blends into the art of living and becomes, in fact, the education of human love."[54] This is axiomatic for Merton: Life and love—not what we are prone to place between us and them—are the one measure.

With no less than life and love as the basic measure, Merton avoided interpreting reality according to formula, theory, or ideology, in the same way, as in *Conjectures* or *Day of a Stranger*, that he eschewed personal identification in terms of prejudicial social categories. He steadfastly resisted placing life, including his own, under some false claim. Consequently, he renounced allegiance with that element of the modern mentality which, in his view, insisted on dividing or delimiting reality and the whole person. He spoke for a "unified existence": "The ordinary acts of everyday life—eating, sleeping, walking, etc.," he observed, "become philosophical acts which group the ultimate principles of life in life itself and not in abstraction."[55]

A greater consciousness of life in its wholeness and greater trust in life as Merton understood and exemplified it, rather than more abstract formula, theory, or ideology, or the arbitrary dictates of society, will clearly help guide education aimed at "the formation of the whole person," and more specifically the development of one's personal voice. To this end, openness to and the study of other cultures—not only for their own sake but also for what they can tell us about ourselves and our own assumptions of reality and the origins and effects of our beliefs as reflected in such areas as technology, ethics, and scientific discovery—can serve an important role.

As deep as was Merton's faith in life, it is important to emphasize that he did not invoke "life" indiscriminately; that is, he did not make life itself an abstraction convenient for serving his own purposes. His primary interest was to open others to a more genuine understanding and concrete experience of life. At the same time, there is an unmistakable hint of anarchy in Merton's fidelity to life, a suggestion that life is incompatible with discipline and the institutions of society. Yet, for Merton, fidelity to life was hardly synonymous with freedom from the discipline of social commitment and responsibility or a disavowal of institutions in and of themselves. Quite the contrary, as his own personal identification with others in society suggests, he clearly believed that one who grasped life in its wholeness would be better able to establish a valid, responsible, and fruitful relationship with other persons.

To live as a whole person requires, in Merton's view, a discipline of love undergirding the disciplines of seeing, hearing, and speaking. Thus, even as Merton's voice was motivated by the love of life he affirmed, it was tempered and disciplined by this love, by, therefore, his desire to be faithful and obedient to "God's truth." He recognized that true freedom rested in obedience—that is, in careful listening, in attuning the whole self—to God. His voice originated in and was disciplined by silence, ultimately by the hidden wholeness, and love, and silence of God.

Not unexpectedly, therefore, Merton did not outright disavow structure or authority, organization or institution, or particular programs even as he affirmed life. Essentially, he believed that they could act on behalf of the whole person by striving to provide an ethos open to life and love. Merton's life as a Trappist monk and member of the Catholic Church in part rested on this belief, and in part on what these institutions meant to him in his life of faith.

Merton endeavored to differentiate between what was done purely for the sake of structure, organization, or institution (or the power they represented) and what promoted life and the person. As in the case of technology and ethics, he was aware of the extreme potential of people, in the context of institutions, to develop, sometimes imperceptibly, an inexorable logic of "right," or to make of their institutions ends in themselves and thus to beguile the persons they are ostensibly meant to serve.

Nazi Germany offered Merton the most obvious and calamitous twentieth-century example of the totalitarian potential of the organizational mind on a broad scale. What alarmed him most was the extent to which the perpetrators of the atrocities of the Third Reich could be judged absolutely sane, even by the courts which later tried them. Reviewing the case of Adolf Eichmann's "sanity," he remarked, "We can no longer assume that because a man is 'sane' he is therefore in his 'right mind.' "[56] In elaborating this theme, he suggested that modern society could not consider itself unsusceptible to the highly efficient, rational, perfectly "adjusted" mode of thinking fostered by Nazi totalitarian ideology and rhetoric. He urged that we guard against making a false morality of rationality and efficiency, particularly in the nuclear age.[57]

The Catholic Church and monasticism were no less susceptible to institutional blindness than any other organization, Merton confirmed in a Cold War letter to a priest.[58] Expanding on this point, he asserted that the ends of Christianity would not be served by the strengthening of medieval Church organization, or by making the Church first and foremost a political instrument rather than a spiritual reality. Merton implies in this Cold War letter that when faith is placed first of all in the Church organization, then the organization, rather than the real faith it is meant to embody and foster, will tend to rule; hence, his support of greater openness on the part of the Church, particularly openness to the possibility of collaboration with the "non-Christian and the non-monk."[59] What "it all comes down to," he offered, is "our actual relationship with our brother."[60] To exemplify this central point, Merton referred to the scope own correspondence, which encompassed "South American poets," "a Moslem friend," and "a lot of others here there and everywhere who have nothing to do with Catholicism"—"I need them and they need me. . . . And the bonds that unite us are supremely important."[61]

Merton's perspective on the nature and role of institutions is perhaps best represented by remarks that he made in the context of a discussion on prayer and monastic renewal recorded by Brother David Steindl-Rast in his essay "Man of Prayer": "It's all a matter of rethinking the identity of the institution so that everything is oriented to people. The institution must serve the development of the individual person. And once you've got fully developed people, they can do anything. What count are people and their vocations, not structures and ideas. Let us make room for idiosyncracies. The danger is that the institution becomes an end in itself. What we need are person-centered communities, not institution-centered ones."[62] Merton recounts familiar themes that strongly implicate the educational institution dedicated to "the formation of the whole person." The institution must serve the whole person, helping to prepare the person for autonomous relationship. This fundamental purpose implies openness as much on the part of the people involved in some "official" way with the institution as on the part of those it is meant to serve.

Having characteristically brought the focus of discussion to the level of the person and personal relationship, Merton did not then offer a set of guidelines and procedures aimed at ensuring a certain quality of person-centeredness in institutions or enabling disaffected members to effect a change in this direction. His contribution would be in clarifying perspective based on personalistic values, not in devising programs which in themselves, in his view, often developed into examples of impersonal institutionalism. Hence, when faced with the inevitable question of how one should act in an institution considered unresponsive to personal need and growth, he tried to clarify what it meant to be a person in that situation, stressing the importance of distinguishing the injustices of the "system" from the actual persons involved. This particular question, along with many of its variations, was pressed on Merton by a group of fifteen cloistered nuns struggling for greater freedom in determining their community life in the context of their religious order in 1967. Merton was leading a conference and retreat for them at Gethsemani.[63] Typically, he did not provide an "answer." "The system has abuses," Merton noted in a general way, "[but] well-meaning people. . . . The only solution I can see is you have to have charity for these people. They are people, too. It's like these friends of mine that are preaching to the Klan because the Klan are people, too."[64] Merton also suggested that there was "no harm of open criticism" when confronting a "faceless system," but that one should avoid getting into the "machinery" of the system unless it is generally agreed to be absolutely necessary. In a remark which recalls his own decision to distribute his Cold War Letters, he suggested that one can go ahead and do what is right in those cases when the "machinery" need not be involved, particularly in a system of injustice.

Merton is careful to clarify this latter point. Characteristically, he emphasizes that "there's always the question of looking and seeing for yourself, 'Am I in the truth?' " Merton implies that there is a rigorous process of questioning involved when one decides to "part company" with authority. Speaking especially to the ecclesiastical and monastic situation, he said, "If the superior is wrong, maybe you're accountable, too. . . . [This] makes it a whole lot tougher! . . . There is this question of being aware. . . . You can't just take anything automatically."[65] He thus confirms the importance of questioning oneself as well as the disturbing practice of the institution, uncovering as much as possible the roots of one's own position in relation to the other, and recognizing in the two possible points of commonality as well as difference. Merton intimates the importance of "dialectical thinking" involving the position of authority and the view supported by one's own conscience as an important part of this process. One does not simply stand in opposition but develops understanding in a dialectic of openness and response; Merton implies the necessity of recognizing that there is an "other," another person, within the framework of institutional dissent and conflict. He notes in this vein the distinction between "living up to the letter of the rule [a legalistic mentality]" and "loving" in determining where one will stand.

The points that Merton emphasized in this particular conference at Gethsemani were highlighted on a more personal level when the question of dissent arose within some sphere of the ecclesiastical institution. Merton's response to a letter from Daniel Berrigan is a case in point. Berrigan informed Merton of his inclination to go ahead and take part in a civil rights demonstration in Birmingham, Alabama, in spite of being denied this permission by his order's superiors. Responding in June of 1963, Merton identified several aspects of Berrigan's proposed position wanting clarification. "Most important of all," he noted, "you do have to consider the continuity of your work as a living unit . . . [and have] an exceptionally grave reason and a rather evident sign that this is required precisely of *you*."[66] Merton asked, in other words, that Berrigan consider the effect his single action would have on his work (primarily teaching and writing) that up to that moment had been vitally important and fruitful, and whether, therefore, in acting contrary to church as well as civil authority, he might be giving up his chance to continue work more important in the long run. In this instance, Merton was suggesting that Berrigan's voice of conscience might be better heard without carrying through the action conscience, unlike the institution, seemed to compel. Interpreted more broadly, Merton was indicating that the decision to act according to conscience in an institutional context, particularly in this ecclesiastical case, involved not only asking "Am I in the truth?" but also demanded that one try to be "aware" of the full dimensions and ramifications of one's action.[67] Merton in no way questioned or downgraded the sincerity of Berrigan's intentions or the importance of the protest on behalf of racial justice. He instead asked those questions which would ensure that whatever action Berrigan took would not simply be a reflex reaction to the position of authority but rather a decision as much as possible based on what he as a unique person in the crisis was most called upon to contribute, on how he personally could best serve the people and truth involved.

As exemplified in his correspondence with Berrigan and his conference remarks to the cloistered nuns,. Merton typically brought discussion involving dissent, authority, or obedience to the level of the person (regardless of religious affiliation) and the experience of relationship. He did not disavow the importance of the church (qua organization) to the world and the individual Christian; he was careful to point out, however, the potential of the church as an institution to blind itself to its own purpose or to be carried away by its own zeal and hope for "success and visible results." Invariably, Merton offered perspective, not answers. At the same time, through his own personal correspondence (which included many members of the church and monastic community), his conferences and counsel, and his efforts to establish a basis for ecumenical, monastic, and East-West religious dialogue, he offered example.

Merton's qualified acceptance of institutions was reflected in a more direct and personal way in his wary response to "movements" and "activity." In spite of his forthright and uncompromising speaking *against,* Merton's speaking *for* only rarely included advocacy of specific actions or groups organized to promote specific causes. Merton's reluctance in this respect, particularly as it involved the peace movement (with which he was perhaps most closely identified in the sixties), stemmed in part from his practical concern that his life as a monk, and furthermore as a hermit, limited his ability to decide from a clear, firsthand knowledge of facts, and thus to act responsibly. At least as important, however, was his concern for the quality of his vocational witness to the importance of greater and unmediated attentiveness to life and the person. Hence, his own "involvement" tended to occur through his personal correspondence, and through informal, small-scale retreats and conferences at Gethsemani itself.[68]

"The trouble with getting involved in movements, organizations, and their activity," Merton explained in one of his Cold War letters, "is that one gets immersed in things which are by their very nature deceptive because they tend to promise much more than the Lord wants of them."[69] This was a cautionary note Merton sounded often in the 1960s for those who looked to him for guidance in their own efforts to blend conscience, protest, and concrete action. It undoubtedly struck more than a few as conservative, noticeably out of proportion to the extent of Merton's own social criticism in the areas of peace and social justice, as likewise to the depth of his support for efforts at renewal in church and monastery. Yet it was typical and hardly inconsistent of Merton (Merton himself rarely worried about consistency in any event) to express reservation if he felt that fidelity to a "cause" or to activism would obscure basic purpose and perspective; that is, obstruct one's vision of life and the person in the specific context in question.[70]

Protest for Merton did not necessarily imply action. It often meant, instead, clarifying, focusing, and deepening perspective—not so much on the purpose of the organization or cause on behalf of which one was acting (thus tending to make of these an "end in themselves"), or even on the nature and effectiveness of the activities to which one was committed, as on the person or persons, and the quality of their relationship, involved in specific situations.[71] Hence, protest in Merton's view presupposes a certain quality of understanding and perspective on the part of the protester, a basic clarity of vision embracing life, person, and relationship before cause, ideal, or movement. Merton's extensive correspondence with such leaders of the 1960s peace movement as Daniel Berrigan, Dorothy Day, James Forest, and John Heidbrink helped to sustain a dialogue aimed at acquiring such perspective. This correspondence thus serves to help illustrate what nurtures and sustains authenticity of personal voice.

To Dorothy Day, well-known advocate of nonviolence and the poor, and co-founder of *The Catholic Worker* (a group dedicated to pacifism and hospitality for the homeless and unemployed), Merton wrote in 1961 on the vital necessity of distinguishing between "the person" and "the actions and policies attributed to him [or her] and his [or her] group."[72] One's primary interest, in the name of protest or reform, could not simply be the principle or idea one was presumably fighting for. A subtle tyranny was enacted when one aimed first and foremost to inculcate a cherished idea, to get another to submit to the "right" way of thinking. Such an effort ignored the fundamental freedom of the person, in effect subjugating the person to an idea or making of the person an object for conversion.

In his counsel to would-be activists, Merton stressed recognizing and acting on behalf of the person who was somehow implicated in the protest *against*. Protest against actions or policies, Merton advised, as in the case of the nuns cited above, but strive above all to open and deepen the experience of relationship as persons. Strive to struggle for greater openness to truth in the common identity of personhood. "Persons are known not by the intellect alone, not by principles alone," he had written in his letter to Dorothy Day, "but only by love."[73] It is only when "we love the other, the enemy," and begin to understand, with God's help, "who he is and who we are" that we can become open to "the real nature of our duty, and of right action."[74]

Especially in light of his correspondence with those in the peace movement, it becomes clear that Merton was concerned not so much with "action" as with the basis of action; not so much with the activist's central question, "What can we do to most effectively achieve our goals?" as with the contemplative's "Who are we who are acting?" It was to the person in each case that he endeavored to speak and respond. It was the person— quite apart from the particular point of disagreement—with whom he sought to identify, and whom, above all, he must love. It was only in knowing the other as person that one could discover oneself as an actor; for self-discovery and discovery of the other as person is a necessary dialectical process in the formation of the whole person, and for the fruitful participation of the whole person in community life.

Whether involving himself, social activists, or members of his church and monastic community, Merton, in voice and example, clearly sought to deepen awareness of life, the whole person, and what it meant to *be* (not necessarily *act*) in each specific context. It was first of all from the understanding of "being" ("who he is and who we are" as he wrote to Dorothy Day) that authentic voice and "right action" would likely develop.

In accordance with Merton's view, action, like the voice of moral protest, can be said to originate paradoxically in silence. It emerges from the silence (not simply passive quietude) in which one becomes conscious of oneself as a whole person, as being, and experiences to some extent the fullness of life, the "hidden wholeness" of God. "Activity is just one of the normal expressions of life," Merton writes in *No Man Is an Island*.[75] It does not, therefore, in and of itself define life or the person. Hence, action, or at least "right action," can be viewed as an expression of wholeness, of the whole person. Action and inaction (in the sense of attentiveness in silence) are thus mutually inclusive, complementary facets of wholeness and of the whole person, each implying and fulfilling the other in a dialectical fashion. To recall Merton's analogous observation regarding music: "[It] is pleasing not only because of the sound, but because of the silence in it. . . . If we twist our lives out of shape in order to fill every corner with action and experience God will silently withdraw from our hearts and leave us empty."[76]

When, in November of 1964, Merton helped gather an ecumenical group for a retreat at Gethsemani Abbey focused on the question of religious dissent and commitment he not surprisingly advocated "The Spiritual Roots of Protest" as the principal theme of the meeting.[77] He prepared a brief mimeographed handout describing the purpose of the retreat in accordance with this theme: "What we are seeking is not the formulation of a program but a deepening of roots. Roots in the 'ground' of all being, in God."[78] Merton's emphasis was typical: The group would not concentrate on answering the question of what to do but, especially important given its ecumenical character, on deepening their understanding of who they were. Having identified some common ground in this respect, Merton hoped that the group would then work to clarify perspectives on the basic questions of protest: "Against whom or what? For what? *By what right?* How? Why?"[79] This effort would require above all "openness"; by implication, a commitment to listening and an "innocent" voice; least of all, the simple defense or imposition of one's point of view. Merton wrote in his mimeographed "Notes" that "it would help if in our meetings we could show our various ways of answering these questions, thus helping one another attain new perspectives. We can help one another to a new *openness.* . . . We will think, speak, and act as brothers."[80]

In his description of the purpose of the meeting, Merton exemplified his deep belief that the voice of protest and the call to action were grounded first of all in being. His sense of the desirable nature of discussion reflected his emphasis on honest and disciplined openness as a prerequisite for speaking and acting in protest. Without a genuine commitment to openness, without a willingness to create room for attaining new perspectives by questioning their very *ways* of thinking about the fundamental facets of protest, without, finally, recognizing themselves as persons ("brothers" in this context) struggling together for an authentic moral response (not simply an effective one), then the authenticity of their voice of protest would itself be open to question.[81]

Given Merton's focus on deepening the roots of protest, it is understandable that he was hesitant to support in the peace movement what he described to James Forest as "provocative action," that is, action which challenges *over and above* the simple question of conscience that is involved."[82] Such action would as likely evoke an aggressive response as a new openness and thus increase the possibility of deeper division. When he did support "provocative witness," as in the case of two specific draft card burnings, it was only because it testified to the morally unconscionable and unjust dimension of the law in question.[83] Action in these cases was a matter of disciplined witness, not simply action for the sake of personal provocation alone. When simply provocative, action was divorced from being, from conscience, from truth. Action which demanded results to vindicate the righteousness of the person and the cause above and beyond the truth and persons involved was spurious. One could confront with a witness to the truth but must strive to avoid intentional provocation; work, in other words, for openness, wholeness, unity on the part of the persons involved. "The job," he wrote to Forest at the end of 1965, "is to get a hearing, a real hearing."[84]

Merton's faith in life and in the wholeness and fullness of being of each person motivated and molded his own voice of protest and tempered his counsel to others. Significant as an illustration of his emphasis on the importance of interpersonal openness in attaining new insight, Merton put the question of action in clearest perspective in a personal letter—full of sympathetic counsel—to James Forest, on February 21, 1966:

> Do not depend on the hope of results. When you are doing the sort of work you have taken on . . . you may have to face the fact that your work will be apparently worthless and even achieve no result at all, if not perhaps results opposite to what you expect. As you get used to this idea, you start more and more to concentrate not on the results but on the value, the rightness, the truth of the work itself. And there too a great deal has to be gone through, as gradually you struggle less and less for an idea and more and more for specific people. The range tends to narrow down, but it gets much more real. In the end . . . it is the reality of personal relationships that saves everything. . . . I am nauseated by [words] . . . ideals and with causes. . . .
>
> The big results are not in your hands or mine, but they suddenly happen and we can share in them; but there is no point in building

our lives on this personal satisfaction, which may be denied us and which after all is not that important.

The next step in the process is for you to see that your own thinking about what you are doing is crucially important. You are probably striving to build yourself an identity in your work and your witness. . . . That is not the right use of your work. All the good that you will do will come not from you but from the fact that you have allowed yourself, in the obedience of faith, to be used by God's love.

The great thing after all is to live, not to pour out your life in the service of a myth: and we turn the best things into myths. If you can get free of the domination of causes and just serve Christ's truth. . . . The real hope, then, is not in something we think we can do but in God who is making something good out of it in some way we cannot see.

Merton concluded, "Enough of this . . . it as at least a gesture."[85]

As reflected poignantly in his letter to Forest, and more broadly in his social protest, his speaking for a renewed understanding of traditional monastic and contemplative life, his affirmation of life, person, and relationship, and his personal correspondence, Merton's personal voice points to several basic qualities and characteristics of the voice of the whole person. These include most notably: authenticity and innocence originating in silence and witnessing to what is real and whole, what is life. Most importantly, authentic voice is the articulate and creative expression of love and truth.

THE VOICE OF TRUTH

According to Merton's understanding, "truth" is expressed in the various existential dimensions of life, having to do with things and persons and their unity in "the hidden ground of love," God. "Truth," insofar as it involves things, refers to their whole actuality and unique identity. Insofar as it refers to the identity of things in their totality, truth can only be apprehended. In comparison, scientific or descriptive explanations of things can reveal something of their particularities and qualities but can do no more than approximate or intimate their whole, living, and concrete truth. Merton suggests in this respect that what science provides is "provisional truth." But it is only in grasping the whole that our understanding enters the broader realm of wisdom: "Wisdom embraces and includes science by attaining to the ultimate, hidden, and definitive truth which is believed rather than known and which is the ground of provisional and changing certitudes."[86] The provisional truth that science provides may broaden one's understanding of the material world and support the attainment of wisdom, while the certainty of wisdom may enable one to more fully appreciate the particularities of things illuminated by science. Science and wisdom in this sense are distinct but hardly unrelated ways of understanding reality, science different in approach and expressing in part what is known as whole by inner experience and conviction.

"Truth" is also "incarnate" in the person, that is, the whole person, the true, indivisible self.[87] Like the truth of things, the incarnate truth that is the person can be intuited, apprehended, and recognized in love. It is in this sense that truth is "known"—on a whole, deeply personal (subjective) and experiential basis (as when Merton writes to Dorothy Day that "persons [can only be] . . . known . . . by love."). Finally, Merton also recognizes the "definitive" truth, the living presence of God intimated by things, transcendent, yet immanent in the person. This is the living Truth, the Truth in which we subsist, and by which we are able to know truth.[88] As Merton understood them, these dimensions of truth form the basis for understanding the "voice of truth," and for every effort at attaining to truth (e.g., the "experimental" mode of science) which can be described as more provisional in nature. How do these dimensions of truth relate to the development of personal voice in the formation of the whole person?

One's capacity for speech is inseparably joined to one's capacity to know the truth. Our capacity to form, interiorly, a word which expresses our relationship to reality is "a spiritual activity . . . centered around our capacity for truth, our capacity to apprehend the truth, and to communicate it," Merton suggested during one of his Gethsemani conferences.[89] In *Conjectures of a Guilty Bystander,* he writes similarly of "our inborn natural sense of the *logos* [the divine word], our love for reasonable expression, our healthy delight in it."[90] His comments suggest the critical importance of awakening to this capacity in ourselves and of recognizing it as an inherent part of our human being. The capacity to speak the truth is one expression of our whole selves (linked to our capacity to appreciate natural beauty) and ultimately our being in God. Merton explains, "In a certain way my word is myself; when I form an interior word about a situation, that word is *me* [italics mine] in relation to that situation."[91] Merton's understanding of the inherent nature of our capacity for speech also suggests the importance of learning to abandon or act in spite of fears which prevent us from speaking what is true. Merton suggests in *Conjectures* that our fears and mistrust originate in our propensity to doubt ourselves and to make of our doubting a confirmation of our inability; thus doubting becomes a measure (albeit a false one) of what in ourselves we consider real.[92] Learning to trust in the ability to know and communicate the truth will clearly be an essential aspect of education involving the formation of the whole person.

Merton maintains that we have learned to mistrust words such as "truth" itself, and "love," "honor," "justice," and "goodness."[93] These concepts "have become sick and rotten to us, not because they are defiled, but because we are." He urges, "Nevertheless, we must dare to think what we mean and simply make clear statements of what we intend."[94] We must attend to our "external" words and think about what we are saying so that our words might conform more readily and fully to their interior origin.[95] Only with this effort will our words be more what they should be—authentically our own, representing our whole selves, thus less susceptible in origin to what is arbitrarily imposed and accepted from without, or the mistrust and doubt that lie within.

The necessity of learning to speak the truth is not at all to suggest that it can be formulated as an objective and then acquired through some efficient, manufactured means. As in the effort to learn to see and hear, the ability to speak the truth requires an interior discipline of openness, attentiveness, and responsiveness. "If we really sought truth we would begin slowly and laboriously to divest ourselves one by one of all our coverings of fiction and delusion," Merton writes in *Conjectures*.[96] Openness implies a recognition of our limitation, our prejudices, our fears, our capacity to delude ourselves; it suggests, as well, a willingness to submit "to what is more than

man." Merton assures us that our true freedom consists paradoxically in this type of submission, which is nothing more than
the letting go of the false self.[97] Only if we relinquish the desire
for control born of fear, if we forbear defining the world solely
in terms of ourselves (in both a personal and ethnocentric
sense), and if we disaffirm the use of power as a way to assert
our reality will we be free to accept and embrace the truth as
whole persons.

In the sense developed here, speaking the truth is not a matter of articulating ideas, concepts, or abstractions which are
held to be true. It is rather the creative, articulated response to
the truth that one, in openness, personally apprehends. To attempt to instill truth—to indoctrinate—is thus to place another's free, creative, personal ability to apprehend the truth in
bondage and to debase the whole person. In order for each
person to discern and recognize their true relation to a situation
("my word . . . is *me* in relation to that situation"), what each
needs most is "space"—room to recollect and focus "me" in
relation to a situation or in response to an essential question;
space to allow interior words to form in the realm of one's silent
wholeness.[98] Precisely the opposite of indoctrination, what is
needed in order to ensure that educational experience involves
the whole person is the opportunity for attentiveness to the
origin of words—implying recollection and silence.

When Merton urged "openness" on the part of participants in
"The Spiritual Roots of Protest" retreat he hosted at Gethsemani, it can be inferred that he was seeking to establish a space
in which participants individually and collectively would be better able to receive a new perspective, thus a "space" in which
prejudice would be minimized and openness to a new and deeper response to truth made possible. Likewise, when he asked
that retreatants try to articulate their "ways" of thinking about
the questions of protest, it can be inferred that he was hoping to
heighten awareness of the interior origin and formulation of
their words and consequently to deepen their consciousness of
the truth and integrity of their views. Remarking in a letter to
peace activist John Heidbrink that "I think we were in contact
with reality and truth in a way that is not met with every day,"
Merton evidently felt that his hopes for the conference were at
least partially fulfilled.[99] In order to be fruitful, the personal

struggle to ascertain truth or the path of moral action will be joined fruitfully with others in a dialectic of openness and response, and of silence and voice. Whether in a broad communal context or formal educational setting, this dialectic will be necessary in order for dialogue to take place. This point will be elaborated in the next chapter.

Merton writes in *No Man Is an Island* that "our need for truth is inescapable."[100] Since we first of all "apprehend" the truth rather than deduce it, truth can be said to have a reality independent of, yet comprehensible by, our power of reason. Truth, in this sense, as already noted, refers especially to things; "Truth, in things, is their reality," Merton explains. He adds that "in our minds it is the conformity of our knowledge with the things known. In our words, it is the conformity of our words to what we think. In our conduct, it is the conformity of our acts to what we are supposed to be."[101] Hence, the truth which can be known can also be integrated into our voice and action. Merton accentuates this point: "Objective truth is a reality that is found both within and outside ourselves, to which our minds can be conformed. We must know this truth, and we must manifest it by our words and acts."[102] Knowing the truth is thus akin to disciplining oneself to see, hear, and speak more attuned to reality. Living according to the truth entails becoming more attuned to the origin of both our words and actions. It was this kind of truthful living that Merton strove to establish as the essential basis for the peace movement and, indeed, as the basis for the life of the whole person.[103]

Merton writes in *Conjectures* that "there is an objective moral good, a good which corresponds to the real value of being, which brings out and confirms the inner significance of our lives when we obey its norms."[104] When we begin, in other words, to understand better who we are as whole persons, then we will live more in accordance with the truth and reality. Our obedience to the norms of objective moral good "integrates us into the whole living movement and development of the cosmos, it brings us into harmony with all the rest of the world, it situates us in our place."[105]

"We make ourselves real," Merton remarks in *No Man Is an Island*, "by telling the truth."[106] One might add that we become real because truth itself is real; our speaking it, therefore, represents that we have become identified with what is real, that we in fact love what is real. As Merton writes, "[Truth] lives and is embodied in [persons] and things that are real. . . . The secret of sincerity is . . . to be sought . . . in a love for real people and real things—a love for God apprehended in the reality around us."[107] The implication is that our "knowing" (our capacity to apprehend the truth) involves our whole selves; thus it is not so much a cognitive activity as an experiential and connatural one which is possible because the capacity for truth itself is rooted in our reality as persons. Knowing the truth in this way signifies that we have become more closely attuned to external reality and to the reality of our own wholeness and the "hidden wholeness" of life itself. This kind of knowing is possible because we also are whole, also life, and united with life in love ("the hidden ground of love"). Merton might suggest that what we need if we are to grow as whole persons in modern society is to learn to know and speak the truth that is as close to ourselves as our own whole being.

Notes

1. Merton, "Letter to an Innocent Bystander," in *Raids*, pp. 53-62; Hans Christian Andersen, "The Emperor's New Clothes," in *Eighty Fairy Tales* (New York: Pantheon, 1976), pp. 64-68.

2. Merton, "Letter to an Innocent Bystander," in *Raids*, p. 62.

3. For an analogous discussion in the context of Merton's thoughts on nonviolence, see Merton, "Blessed Are the Meek: The Christian Roots of Nonviolence," in *The Nonviolent Alternative*, p. 216.

4. Referring to Merton's as yet publically restricted journals, Michael Mott presents Merton's analysis (1961) of his own authenticity as a bystander; Mott, *The Seven Mountains of Thomas Merton*, p. 365; see also Merton's introduction to *Seeds of Destruction*, p. xi.

5. Merton, "Letter to an Innocent Bystander," in *Raids*, p. 61; cf., Merton, *Opening the Bible*, p. 92.

6. Merton, *Conjectures*, pp. 5-6.

7. See Conference Tape 265B, "Growing Up Beyond Social World," February 18, 1968 (Louisville, Ky., Bellarmine College: Thomas Merton Studies Center, unpublished tape).

8. Merton, *No Man*, p. 195.

9. Mott, *The Seven Mountains of Thomas Merton*, p. 368; see also, as noted above (note 4), p. 365.

10. Quoted in Mott, *The Seven Mountains of Thomas Merton*, p. 368; see Merton, "Cold War Letters," #1, p. 2.

11. Mott, *The Seven Mountains of Thomas Merton*, p. 368.

12. Ibid., p. 369.

13. Merton, "Cold War Letters," preface.

14. Mott, *The Seven Mountains of Thomas Merton*, p. 623 (note 228).

15. Mott, *The Seven Mountains of Thomas Merton*, p. 380; Merton, *No Man*, p. 121; Merton to James Forest, February 21, 1966, in Shannon, ed., *The Hidden Ground of Love*, pp. 294-297.

16. Merton to Dorothy Day, August 23, 1961, in Shannon, ed., *The Hidden Ground of Love*, p. 139.

17. Merton occasionally circumvented possible censorship of incoming letters by advising others (such as Daniel Berrigan and his young friend from California, Suzanne Butorovich) to mark "conscience matter" on their letters.

18. See, for example, Merton's remarks to Wilbur Ferry, January 18, 1962, in Shannon, ed., *The Hidden Ground of Love*, p. 204.

19. Ibid.

20. Mott, *The Seven Mountains of Thomas Merton*, p. 371.

21. Daggy, ed., *Introductions*, pp. 45-46.

22. Merton, *No Man*, p. 127.

23. See, for example, Merton, "Ecumenism and Renewal," in *Contemplation in a World of Action*, pp. 196-197, and "THE POORER MEANS: A Meditation on Ways to Unity," *Sobornost* (Winter-Spring, 1966), pp. 74-79.

24. Merton to James Forest, April 29, 1962, in Shannon, ed., *The Hidden Ground of Love*, p. 267.

25. Merton, *Seeds*, p. xi.

26. Ibid.

27. Ibid., p. xiv.

28. Merton to James Forest, April 29, 1962, in Shannon, ed., *The Hidden Ground of Love*, p. 267.

29. Merton to Daniel Berrigan, June 25, 1963, in Shannon, ed., *The Hidden Ground of Love*, p. 79. Indicative of this as part of a growing conviction for Merton are his final public remarks to his fellow monks in Bangkok: "The monk belongs to the world but the world belongs to him insofar as he has dedicated himself totally to liberation from it in order to liberate it"; Merton, "Marxism and Monastic Perspectives," Appendix VII, in *Asian Journal*, p. 341.

30. See, for example, Merton to Dom Francis Decroix, August 21, 1967, in Shannon, ed., *The Hidden Ground of Love*, pp. 154-158, in which he provides his sample of a "message from a contemplative to the world."

31. Thomas Merton, "Contemplation and Dialogue," in *Mystics and Zen Masters* (New York: Farrar, Straus & Giroux, 1967), p. 204.

32. Daggy, ed., *Introductions*, p. 46.

33. See, for example, Gordon C. Zahn, "The Spirituality of Peace," in *The Legacy of Thomas Merton*, ed. Brother Patrick Hart, (Kalamazoo, Mich.: *Cistercian Publications*, 1986), pp. 199-215.

34. Merton, "Letter to an Innocent Bystander," in *Raids*, p. 61.

35. Merton, *Thoughts*, p. 78.

36. Merton, "Atlas and the Fatman," in *Raids*, pp. 106-107.

37. Merton, "The Pasternak Affair," in *Disputed Questions*, pp. 7-8.

38. Boris Pasternak, *Dr. Zhivago* (New York: Signet Books, 1958), p. 325.

39. Ibid., see p. 325.

40. Merton, "The Pasternak Affair," in *Disputed Questions*, pp. 3-67.

41. Pasternak, *Dr. Zhivago*, p. 39.

42. See, for example, Merton's comments on science and wisdom in "The Need for a New Education," *Contemplation in a World of Action*, p. 203.

43. Thomas Merton, *Ishi Means Man* (Greensboro, N.C.: Unicorn Press, 1968), pp. 69-70.

44. Ibid., pp. 58-59.

45. Ibid., p. 58.

46. Ibid., especially, pp. 70-71.

47. Merton to Wilbur Ferry, September 24, 1967, in Shannon, ed., *The Hidden Ground of Love*, p. 235.

48. Thomas Merton, *The Geography of Lograire* (New York: New Directions, 1968), p. 1.

49. See discussion in George Woodcock, *Thomas Merton, Monk and Poet* (Edinburgh: Canongate, 1978), p. 180.

50. Merton, *Conjectures*, p. 75.

51. Ibid., p. 253; see also, Merton, "The Need for a New Education," in *Contemplation in a World of Action*, p. 203.

52. Merton, "The Need for a New Education," in *Contemplation in a World of Action*, p. 203.

53. Merton, "Ethics," in *Love and Living*, p. 112.

54. Ibid.

55. Merton, *Conjectures*, p. 292.

56. Merton, "A Devout Meditation in Memory of Adolf Eichmann," in *Raids*, p. 47.

57. Ibid.

58. Addressed anonymously in Merton, *Seeds*, pp. 318-326.

59. Ibid., p. 322.

60. Ibid., p. 324.

61. Ibid.

62. David Steindl-Rast, "Man of Prayer," in Hart, ed., *Thomas Merton / Monk*, p. 85.

63. Conference Tape #289B, "Authority, Progress," December (?), 1967 (Louisville, Ky., Bellarmine College: Thomas Merton Studies Center, unpublished tape); Merton was very impressed with the group; as he remarked in a letter to Suzanne Butorovich, "Just had a wonderful time with fifteen cloistered nuns who came here for a sort of retreat and conference deal to study 'problems'. . . they were all very keyed up and alive and it was a groovy experience; they are smart, too." Merton to Suzanne Butorovich, December 9, 1967 (Thomas Merton Studies Center).

64. Conference Tape #289B, "Authority, Progress."

65. Ibid.

66. Merton to Daniel Berrigan, June 25, 1963, in Shannon, ed., *The Hidden Ground of Love*, p. 77.

67. See also Merton's letter to Daniel Berrigan, October 14, 1966, in Shannon, ed., *The Hidden Ground of Love*, pp. 89-91.

68. Merton was a sponsor of the Catholic Peace Fellowship, beginning in 1964, but considered that a largely symbolic statement, since he could not be part of practical decision making; still he was uncomfortable with the responsibility his sponsorship implied, particularly after a member of *The Catholic Worker*, Roger La Porte, immolated himself in front of the United Nations building on November 11, 1965. His letters of November 19 and December 3, 1965, to James Forest, illustrate his ambivalence (See Shannon, ed., *The Hidden Ground of Love*, pp. 287-290.)

69. Merton, *Seeds*, p. 324.

70. Regarding the question of his own consistency, Merton wrote in his journal (January 25, 1964): "My ideas are always changing, always moving around one center, and I am always seeing that center from somewhere else. Hence, I will always be accused of inconsistency. But I will no longer be there to hear the accusation"; Merton, *Vow of Conversation*, p. 19.

71. See Merton, "Blessed Are the Meek," in *The Nonviolent Alternative*, p. 211; Merton mentions "the truth that is incarnate in a concrete human situation, involving living persons."

72. Merton to Dorothy Day, December 20, 1961, in Shannon, ed., *The Hidden Ground of Love*, p. 141.

73. Ibid.

74. Ibid.

75. Merton, *No Man*, p. 172.

76. Ibid., pp. 127-128ff.

77. Participants at the retreat/conference included John Yoder, A. J. Muste, and Daniel Berrigan.

78. Thomas Merton, "Spiritual Roots of Protest," (Louisville, Ky., Bellarmine College: Thomas Merton Studies Center, mimeographed notes), p. 1. See also Merton, *The Nonviolent Alternative*, ed. Gordon Zahn, pp. 259-260.

79. Ibid.

80. Ibid.

81. After the retreat, Merton wrote to John Heidbrink, an active member of the peace movement, "I think we were in contact with reality and truth in a way that is not met with every day;" Merton to John Heidbrink, November 26, 1964, in Shannon, ed., *The Hidden Ground of Love*, p. 417. Specifically, Merton noted "the sense of the awful depth and seriousness of the situation" and "a sense of deeper and purer hope, a hope purified of trust in the technological machinery and the 'principalities and powers' at work therein."

82. Merton to James Forest, December 29, 1965, in Shannon, ed., *The Hidden Ground of Love*, p. 291.

83. Ibid., p. 292.

84. Ibid., p. 293.

85. Merton to James Forest, February 21, 1966, in Shannon, ed., *The Hidden Ground of Love*, pp. 294-297.

86. Merton, "Ecumenism and Renewal," in *Contemplation in a World of Action*, p. 190.

87. See "Blessed Are the Meek," in *The Nonviolent Alternative*, p. 211 (see note 71 above).

88. The subjective quality of truth is not, of course, unique to Merton's contemplative perspective but is also inherent in the Christian and other religious faiths. I would draw attention in particular to an illuminating book by one of Merton's friends by correspondence, Abraham Heschel, for illustration: Abraham Heschel, *A Passion for Truth* (New York: Farrar, Straus & Giroux, 1973); Heschel's work is a comparative study of the Christian existentialist, Søren Kierkegaard and the Kotzker, a Jewish spiritual leader of, like Kierkegaard, the nineteenth century. Heschel cites a story about the Kotzker (from the Hasidic tradition—from which Merton often borrowed in his conferences on spiritual questions) which is illustrative here:

There is a story about a learned young man who came to see the Kotzker. No longer young—he was close to thirty—the visitor had never before been to a rebbe.

"What have you done all your life?" the master asked him.

"I have gone through the whole Talmud three times," answered the guest.

"Yes, but how much of the Talmud has gone through you?" Reb Mendl inquired. (p. 107).

89. Conference Tape #135B, "Silence and Making Signs" (Louisville, Ky., Bellarmine College: Thomas Merton Studies Center, unpublished tape).

90. Merton, *Conjectures*, p. 92.

91. Conference Tape #135B, "Silence and Making Signs;" see also Chapter 4 on "Speaking."

92. See Merton, *Conjectures*, p. 92.

93. Ibid.; see also Merton, *No Man*, p. 193.

94. Merton, *Conjectures*, pp. 92-93.

95. Conference Tape 135B, "Silence and Making Signs."

96. Merton, *Conjectures*, p. 68.

97. Ibid., p. 92.

98. I am especially indebted to Henri Nouwen (personal interview, May 2, 1985) and Parker Palmer *(To Know As We Are Known / A Spirituality of Education)* for introducing me to this idea of "space."

99. Merton to John Heidbrink, November 26, 1964, in Shannon, ed., *The Hidden Ground of Love*, p. 417.

100. Merton, *No Man*, p. 189.

101. Ibid.

102. Ibid., p. 190.

103. Merton, "Ecumenism and Renewal," in *Contemplation in a World of Action*, p. 190.

104. Merton, *Conjectures*, p. 119.

105. Ibid.

106. Merton, *No Man*, p. 188.

107. Ibid., p. 198.

6

Communication, Dialogue, and Communion

Just as the discipline of speaking suggests a particular quality of voice, the voice of the whole person implies a particular quality of communication and dialogue.

The origin of voice is interior, its quality subjective in that it expresses a deeply personal experience of something known. The existential and relational nature of this personal experience reflects an epistemology grounded in the reality of being, in one's being united to truth and living reality in the fullness of being, that is, in the hidden wholeness and love of God. The voice of the whole person will be authentic in proportion as it emerges from and expresses this whole quality of knowing. This implies a certain quality of innocence on the part of the person. To speak authentically and thus innocently, the whole person must speak in humble fidelity and response to life, person, and reality; one must strive to speak from an integrity of openness and honest response to a deep, interior experience of knowing the truth or apprehending reality. The "external" words which one voices are as much as possible formulated in conformity to the "interior" words which express one's personal experience in relation to truth or reality; as Merton says, they are the unique, creative expression of "me" (the whole person) in relation to a situation.[1] The effort to speak in accordance with genuine interior response will be a vital sign of the quality of personal communication involved in the formation of the whole person.

COMMUNICATION

Communication will clearly be commensurate with the whole person to the extent that it is an expression of authentic voice. In other words, a genuinely personal communication will in some way convey a deeper, concrete experience of person and life, truth and reality. As Merton declares in one of his Cold War Letters, "Communication must always fulfill one essential condition if it is to exist at all: It must be human, it must have resonances that are deeper than formal statements, declarations, and manifestoes."[2] Communication divorced from its essential interior personal origin will not only serve to distort truth and reality but will alienate the person from his/her inner source of freedom and identity and from reality itself. In the context of society, such impersonal communication will relegate the person to anonymous status as an individual member of the collectivity, as an object in the "mass."

Merton saw much in the content and modes of communication in Western society in conflict with his faith in the inviolate and sacred nature of the person. He saw comparatively little in support of his trust in the deepest levels of human experience and probity and the capacity to know and apprehend the truth. He was concerned particularly with the effects of propaganda, advertising and mass media communication, technology, a narrow scientific worldview, and misappropriated language on personal freedom and judgment and personal relationship to reality. This concern is apparent in much of his writing, especially in *Conjectures of a Guilty Bystander* and the essays, "Symbolism" and "War and the Crisis of Language."[3] He addresses it as well in some of his correspondence and in a conference on "mass communications" that he offered to his fellow monks at Gethsemani Abbey in 1966.[4] Merton explains in *Conjectures* that propaganda distorts communication in two basic ways: by misrepresenting or falsifying the truth and, more subtly and insidiously, by manipulating the truth itself to beguile.[5] In either case, propaganda can create an impression of truth or rationality simply in the *way* information is presented (e.g., in an objective, pseudo-scientific or authoritative manner) thus effectively camouflaging the actual irrationality or meaninglessness of the purportedly sincere message.[6] By creating an impression of irrefutable objectivity through the use of such data as "statistical facts," some forms of propaganda fed what Merton considered a widespread but misguided belief in a positivistic approach as the most credible and acceptable form of truth in social discourse. Propaganda deludes with this kind of false authoritative voice; those who subscribe, or more accurately succumb, to it, once again misjudge the style of the message for its substance. Merton was disturbed most by the pernicious effect of propaganda on the freedom of the person. Propaganda can induce us "to surrender our freedom and self-possession" by creating an "illusion of identity and freedom," he noted.[7] We feel that we are informed, we imagine that we are "real," when in fact we have forfeited our independent thinking and basic freedom to the anonymous "mass mind."[8]

Merton remarks soberly that "there are no innocent victims of propaganda" in modern society. "Propaganda succeeds because [people] want it to succeed."[9] His concern, therefore, does not stem simply from the fact that propaganda is impersonal communication but from our apparent readiness to respond to it as individuals rather than more deeply and independently as whole persons. Merton might say that we need to learn to better recognize and respond to pseudo-authenticity inside as well as outside ourselves even as we strive for authenticity in our own voices.

Merton's discussion of propaganda raises the more general questions of how one distinguishes the false and true in communication and how one becomes accurately informed on social issues so as to make reasoned judgments. While he does not offer definitive answers to these questions, Merton does, in the context of his Gethsemani conference on "mass communications," highlight the importance of asking them. He provides in the process an example of communication that is more genuinely personal and more attuned to life and reality.

"How do you get informed about what the world is? Do you get informed? Do mass communications really inform? If they don't, what do they do? What should you get?" Merton asks in opening his Gethsemani conference on "mass communications" (May 22, 1966).[10] Merton proceeds to emphasize the need for "objective information . . . in a meaningful context" from mass media, yet concludes critically that what we get instead is a "constant trivialization of important things . . . [which] ends up in a trivial view of people and of life, of the nation . . . with people taking nothing seriously or pseudo-seriously."[11] Merton suggests that mass media communication consequently sells but fails to draw readers into any deeper contact with people and reality, fails to generate any sense of commitment or responsibility, or any genuine interior response. "What does this produce? What kind of effect does this have on a person's conscience? What is [his/her] attitude toward life? . . . It really amounts to . . . an attitude of noncommitment to anything. . . . You don't know what to think about anything so leave it alone. . . . People are suspicious of committing themselves to anything."[12]

Drawing on information provided by Wilbur Ferry, his friend and then vice-president of the Center for Democratic Institutions, Merton identifies crucial social situations (e.g., racial tension, the Vietnam War) which he considers were either neglected by the media or reported without serious consideration of their meaning in human terms. "The real meaning of the race problem was not discovered by the press," Merton points out, "it was brought to the attention of the nation by the Civil Rights movement."[13] Merton also cites the failure of mass communications to portray the real "poverty" ("the invisible poor") of the United States during the sixties as another example of its unreliability and lack of "care."

Merton does not identify reliable sources of information in this particular conference so much as characterize what reliable information would be like and stress the importance of looking for it and obtaining it ("we should do a study about what's useful and worth having [in the monastic community]"). In another conference for the Gethsemani community (May 29, 1966), however, he does offer an example of a personal, and what he considered to be a highly credible source of information to illustrate both the "reality" of a "crisis situation" (the Vietnam War) and the quality of communication that a monk could provide in such an instance—the firsthand account of Vietnamese Buddhist monk Thich Nhat Hanh.[14] What distinguishes Nhat Hanh's account, according to Merton, is its whole orientation to peace, and the corresponding focus on people and life rather than on politics, ideology, or power. Nhat Hanh's portrayal brings one closer to the "reality" of the crisis situation, something to which one can relate more deeply than to the "ideas of it you can get out of *Time* [magazine]."[15] Hence, it is not only the realistic and person-oriented nature of Nhat Hanh's form of communication that is important but the quality of personal response that it is likely to evoke. Able to relate more strongly to the personal reality of the situation, one can then better respond on behalf of people and life and not to "certain thoughts about certain kinds of things." Nhat Hanh and small groups of his friends themselves demonstrate this kind of response in their nonpolitical effort to educate themselves and do something constructive in their war-torn country. This is the whole point for Merton: Nhat Hanh's is a life-affirming response, an outgrowth of reverence for life and people— "and all that can help people to grow."[16]

Nhat Hanh's politically disinterested and personal focus is compelling evidence for Merton of the sincerity and relevance of his voice. Hence subsequent to his meeting with Nhat Hanh at Gethsemani, Merton composed a personal appeal on behalf of his life and work in Vietnam in a short piece entitled, "Nhat Hanh Is My Brother": "[Nhat Hanh] represents the young, the defenseless, the new ranks of youth who find themselves with every hand turned against them except those of the peasants and the poor, with whom they are working. Nhat Hanh speaks truly for the people of Vietnam. . . . Nhat Hanh is my brother . . . [united] in something that is more concrete than an ideal and more alive than a program."[17] Merton's sense of fraternal connection with Nhat Hanh contrasts sharply with the "we-they" perception of Vietnam he suggests is conveyed through an account of the war he read in *Life* magazine while on a medical visit to Louisville, Kentucky, in 1965, about a year before his Gethsemani conference on mass communications. "The whole picture," he writes in his journal, "is one of an enormously equipped and self-complacent white civilization in combat with a huge sprawling colored and mestizo world. . . . The implicit assumption behind it . . . is that 'we' are the injured ones. We are trying to keep peace and order and 'they,' abetted by Communist demons, are simply causing confusion and chaos with no reasonable motives whatever. Dealing with all these inferior peoples becomes a technical problem, something like pest extermination. . . . America is oversimplifying all the questions, reducing them to terms which make sense to us only and to no one else. . . . Hence, a fatal breakdown of communication, which is the worst problem today."[18] There can be no real communication where there is no personal recognition, no effort to enable the other to stand forth as person or to see the reality of the other's situation and, potentially, the inadequacy of one's own preconceptions. Without real communication we are likewise limited in how and to what we will respond; hence, again, the significance of Nhat Hanh.

"We *are* the world," Merton writes in a brief exposition called "World." "The question, then, is not to speculate about how we are to contact the world . . . but how to validate our relationship, give it a fully honest and human significance, and make it truly productive and worthwhile."[19] Nhat Hanh clearly offered Merton a powerful personal example, in the context of a "crisis situation," of a concrete way to "validate our relationship" with the world. He felt, in contrast, the emptiness and superficiality of mass communication in his own society, the sad and ironic attenuation of human connection and commitment in the midst of a broadening mass communications network. Merton often referred to a narrowly defined scientific and technological worldview as a delimiting factor in fully human communication. He cautions in his essay "Symbolism" that modern science and technology can erode our deepest sensibilities of relationship with reality, and thus our capacity for life, if they become accepted as the symbol for communication, as, essentially, both the mode and meaning of communication.

> In technological society, in which the means of communication and signification have become fabulously versatile, and are at the point of an even more prolific development, thanks to the computer with its inexhaustible memory and its capacity for immediate absorption and organization of facts, the very nature and use of communication itself becomes unconsciously symbolic. Though he now has the capacity to communicate anything, anywhere, instantly, man finds himself with *nothing to say*. Not that there are not many things he could communicate, or should attempt to communicate. He should, for instance, be able to meet with his fellow man and discuss ways of building a peaceful world. He is incapable of this kind of confrontation. Instead of this, he has intercontinental missiles. . . . This is the most sophisticated message modern man has, apparently, to convey

to his fellow man. It is, of course, a message about himself, and his inability to come to terms with life.[20].

Narrowly construed, science and technology can build and support an illusion of separation from, or of standing over and against reality. As a consequence, what becomes most meaningful is what will function to support this illusion (more and even better technology); the idea of function itself becomes an integral part of the illusion. In this narrow worldview, the "world" is more or less meant to be appropriated—science will "gather quantitative data about the physical universe" and provide the objective knowledge to "serve the practical needs of technology."[21] "Knowledge," meanwhile, "is not a knowledge of reality but a knowledge of knowledge."[22] Meaning is expressed by external results within this synthetic construct of knowledge, making of the world less and less a living reality and more and more a self-enclosed "artificial synthesis" in which subjective, interior meaning has been supplanted by something objectified and externalized.[23]

Merton did not repudiate technology and science but feared the potential of their misuse or overuse to enhance the "will to power" at the expense of authentic communication and relationship to reality: "Naturally, the advance of science and technology is irreversible and man now has to come to terms with himself in his new situation. He cannot do so if he builds an irrational and unscientific faith on the absolute and final objectivity of scientific knowledge of nature."[24] What is Merton suggesting in saying that "man now has to come to terms with himself in his new situation"? On one level he is clearly emphasizing the importance of asking ourselves how, in an era of rapidly expanding technology and scientific knowledge, we will go about validating our inherent relationship with the world, giving it "a fully honest and human significance" and making it "truly productive and worthwhile." How, in other words, with the apparent change in our external relationship to the world wrought by technology and science, will we continue to recognize and sustain our actual relationship? How will we maintain a subjective, authentically human perspective and promote a quality of life commensurate with the interior freedom and growth of the whole person? In what will our communication, our knowledge, our understanding really consist and what will it influence us to be? What will be our wisdom?

Merton explains in his essay "Symbolism" that there are creative and living symbols which evoke a deeper consciousness of integration, of unity in the ontological reality of being, and of "human love" and "contemplative truth."[25] By "symbols," Merton means "living signs of creative integration and inner life." These living signs in themselves contain "a structure which in some way makes us aware of the inner meaning of life and of reality itself," thereby encouraging "acceptance of [our] own center, [our] own ontological roots in a mystery of being that transcends . . . individual ego."[26] The "symbol," in contrast to the "sign," goes beyond "practicality and purpose" and "cause and effect" (the values promoted by technology). In the symbol communication is in essence fused with "communion." "The purpose of the symbol . . . is not to increase the quantity of our knowledge and information but to deepen and enrich the *quality* of life itself by bringing [us] into communion with the mysterious sources of vitality and meaning, of creativity, love, and truth, to which [we] cannot have direct access by means of science and technique. The realm of symbol is the realm of wisdom in which [we] find truth not only in and through objects but in [ourselves] and [our] life."[27] Merton mentions two types of symbols: The "social" variety, through which one "can make the common good really [one's] own," and the religious symbol, by means of which "the person can enter into communion, not only with [others] and with all creation, but with God."[28] Symbols of this quality are clearly evocative, life-giving and life-affirming.

Although he does not discuss it explicitly in "Symbolism," Merton illustrates elsewhere his belief in the power of symbols created in art and literature to evoke a whole experience of life and consequently a fundamental sense of meaning which he suggests deepens or renews our consciousness as whole persons.[29] He notes in his wide-ranging essay on "Wisdom and Initiation in William Faulkner" that "creative writing and imaginative criticism provide a privileged area for wisdom in the modern world. At times one feels they do so even more than current philosophy and theology."[30] Merton's descriptive term for this quality of creative expression is "sapiential" (denoting wisdom).[31] Among those whom he considers "sapiential writers" are T. S. Eliot, Boris Pasternak (see comments on *Dr. Zhivago* in previous chapter), and William Butler Yeats; among those who express what he means, he cites Catholic philosopher Jacques Maritain (*Creative Intuition in Art and Poetry*), Zen scholar D. T. Suzuki (*Zen and Japanese Culture*), and poet William Carlos Williams (*In the American Grain*).[32]

Merton explains that the sapiential approach "seeks to apprehend [the person's] value and destiny in their global and even ultimate significance."[33] To this end, the sapiential approach depends on poetic myth, or religious and archetypal symbols which "are not directed so much at the understanding and control of things as at [the person's] own understanding of [self]." Awakened by symbols, "sapiential awareness deepens our communion with the concrete."[34] Merton offers the "spiritual intuition" of Ike McCaslin, Faulkner's main character in *Go Down, Moses*, as an example of Faulkner's use of the sapiential, as he does the main characters in Faulkner's *The Wild Palms*. Merton's treatment of these sapiential themes points to their importance in the education of the whole person. The opportunity to encounter symbols through art and literature, in addition to opportunities to study the mythic traditions of different cultures and engage in more direct forms of authentic communication, will clearly serve the formation of the whole person.[35]

Common to all the areas which affect quality of communication, and consequently of great importance to the ability of the person to respond wholly, interiorly, and creatively to the world, are the nature and use of language. Whether in the realms of advertising, politics, art, religion, love, or most destructively, war, the nature and use of language could mean the difference between openness, dialogue, and interior response and tautology, control, and manipulation. Language which no longer conveys, or no longer is intended to convey, any semblance of truth or reality is, in Merton's eyes, "denatured," neither a means of authentic personal communication, nor a signification for or evocation of reality. In propaganda, language is denatured as the instrument of false intention; it is denatured in mass communication insofar as it fosters a trivialized view of and response to life; in the language of a narrow scientific worldview, it is denatured to the extent that it creates an artificial distance between person and truth, person and reality, person and creative, interior response. But language reflects and creates the greatest insensitivity to life and reality and human meaning when it closes off personal engagement, interior response, and dialogue. Merton's examples of this kind of unilateral communication range from advertising to the "sinister jargon of the war mandarins in government offices and military think-tanks."[36] Ultimately, denatured language, as the servant of power (the false self), prepares the way for "war" as a "much more 'sure' means of communication"—at least this is Merton's thesis in a letter to Wilbur Ferry and in his essay, "War and the Crisis of Language."[37]

In advertising, Merton saw an outstanding example of the use of language resulting in closed, meaningless communication; an authoritative *sense* of meaning is conveyed, but the message itself is meaningless. Merton remarks, for example, on a poetic advertisement for a perfume called "Arpège," whose ultimate ontological significance is proven with the inscrutable declaration that "Arpège . . . has Arpège."[38] Merton writes that the poem is "beyond parody. It must stand inviolate in its own victorious rejection of meaning."[39] Its synthetic substitute for meaning is contained in its "logical *structure*"; it is "foolproof tautology, locked tight upon itself, impenetrable, unbreakable, irrefutable. It is endowed with a finality so inviolable that it is beyond debate and beyond reason."[40]

Merton draws a direct parallel between the sense of definitude communicated in advertisements and the cold certitude conveyed in the "sinister jargon of the war mandarins in government offices and military think-tanks." The desensitized, highly practical and efficient language used to discuss the possibility of war becomes the measure of credibility within a "masculine, that is, managerial mode" of thinking, until it in fact controls thinking and becomes the infallible justification for its own use.[41] So manipulated and manipulating, denatured language becomes the handmaiden of power and consequently the preemptor of dialogue; in its "self-enclosed finality" it can ultimately reach no other conclusion than that the "enemy" is actually what it presumes—irrational, intractable, intolerable, and amenable to no other form of suasion than force. Such language, Merton warns, particularly when "given universal currency by the mass media . . . can quickly contaminate the thinking of everybody."[42]

In discussing language and the subtle ease with which it can manipulate and be manipulated, Merton once again demonstrates that his paramount concern is for a quality of communication commensurate with the whole person. To the extent that speech and language express concrete human experience, they will promote greater integrity and openness in communication. Communication will be more "human," will have "resonances that are deeper than formal statements, declarations, and manifestoes," and thus will contribute in education to the formation of the whole person. When we communicate as whole persons, we invite openness and can occasion like response; we lay the groundwork for genuine human dialogue.

DIALOGUE

In one of his Gethsemani conferences, on Sufism, Merton mentions that the normal way of human fulfillment will be through dialogue and community life.[43] Dialogue is one of the most fundamental ways that we have of actualizing our living relationship with others as persons; it is also a way of creatively expressing our relationship and of enhancing our shared relationship to natural reality. Dialogue, then, is neither a matter of discussion, nor an exchange of information, nor least of all a debate but rather a *joint participation*. When we enter into dialogue, we participate more fully in our creative life as whole persons united in the hidden, fertile, creative ground of love. Dialogue, in other words, is at once a fully ontological and communal process.

We can only find ourselves "in and through others," to recall a central message of *No Man Is an Island*.[44] In and through dialogue, we can together become more open to this paradoxical discovery; we can realize ourselves more as whole persons.

Our capacity for dialogue, then, in correspondence with our capacity to form and renew community, inheres in our living relationship as persons united in the ground of being. The importance of dialogue for our lives as whole persons cannot be understood apart from this ontological perspective which embraces self and other. It follows that the effort to create dialogue will not be shaped by ideas or principles, but rather, on a more subjective basis, by recognition of and identification with the other as person, possible only through love. Dialogue will to some extent reflect, affirm, and strengthen this relationship, the actual topic of dialogue notwithstanding. Hence, reflecting the truth of our unity as persons and our mutual, subjective capacity to know this truth, the person will be both the basis for and approach to creating dialogue. On any other basis, or with any other approach, the possibility for creating the transforming dynamic of openness, response, and broader understanding essential to dialogue will be limited, if not extinguished.

Merton articulated the person-oriented basis for and approach to dialogue as part of his effort to apply his profound Christian understanding of the person to the difficult question of how to address issues of peace and social justice with others. He sketched what might be called his philosophy of dialogue in a "Cold War Letter" to Dorothy Day (published in *Seeds of Destruction* in 1964) and incorporated it several years later in one of his most important discussions of the philosophy and practice of nonviolence from a Christian perspective, "Blessed Are the Meek: The Christian Roots of Nonviolence" (1966).[45]

In his letter to Dorothy Day, Merton enters his discussion of the personal basis for dialogue from the perspective of the underlying assumptions of Christian ethics. "The basic thing in Christian ethics," he emphasizes, "is to look at the *person* and not at the *nature*."[46] He suggests that "when we consider 'nature' we consider the general, the theoretical, and forget the concrete, the individual, the personal reality of the one confronting us."[47] Based on the abstract view of "nature," our relation to another is predetermined, closed; we limit our ability to identify with the other as person, as in fact "our other self, . . . as Christ." When "we resort to the impersonal 'law' and 'nature,' " rather than to love, we "*shut out* the person. . . . That is to say we block off the reality of the other, we cut the intercommunication of our nature and his nature, and we consider our own nature with its rights, its claims, its demands. In effect, we are considering *our nature in the concrete* and *his nature in the abstract*. And we justify the evil we do to our brother because he is no longer a brother."[48] To be fully personal, dialogue will require a more humble, open, loving, and, for Merton, more faithful approach:

"To restore communication, to see our oneness of nature with him, and to respect his personal rights, his integrity, his worthiness of love, we have to see ourselves accused along with him, condemned to death along with him, sinking into the abyss with him, and needing, with him, the ineffable gift of grace and mercy to be saved. Then instead of pushing him down, trying to climb out by using his head as a stepping stone for ourselves, we help ourselves to rise by helping him to rise. When we extend our hand to the enemy who is sinking in the abyss, God reaches out for both of us, for it is He first of all who extends our hand to the enemy."[49]

In the philosophy of nonviolence, Merton saw a basis for dialogue compatible with his Christian, spiritual understanding of the person. Its roots in a metaphysic emphasizing spiritual unity and the innate capacity to love and know the truth, and its wisdom based on experience rather than on ideas or "logic" offered the most striking parallels. Merton establishes this common ground in his discussion of Mahatma Gandhi's philosophy in essays entitled "A Tribute to Gandhi" and "Gandhi and the One-Eyed Giant," the introduction to his collection of excerpts from Gandhi's writing (*Gandhi on Nonviolence*);[50] his effort to clarify the Christian basis for nonviolence, particularly in "Blessed Are the Meek: The Christian Roots of Nonviolence," is also relevant. A brief summary here of the points of commonality will broaden and strengthen the foundation for understanding the nature of dialogue commensurate with the whole person thus far presented, and prepare the way for subsequent discussion of the general characteristics of dialogue.

In one of the excerpts from his writing compiled by Merton, Gandhi writes, "Belief in nonviolence is based on the assumption that human nature in its essence is one and therefore unfailingly responds to the advances of love."[51] This statement correlates strongly with Merton's observation in "Blessed Are the Meek" that "Christian nonviolence is not built on a presupposed division but on the basic unity of [humanity]."[52] Nonviolence, in both instances, is not perceived as a means of achieving unity but as the true way of being reflecting unity, since unity is already manifest and able to be experienced in being. Accordingly, the "seat" of nonviolence, in Gandhi's words, "is in the heart, and it must be an inseparable part of our very being."[53]

Martin Luther King in his explanation of the philosophy of nonviolence similarly observes, "At the center of nonviolence stands the principle of love ["agape"]. . . . *agape* means a recognition of the fact that all life is interrelated. All humanity is involved in a single process, and all men are brothers."[54]

Merton suggests in "A Tribute to Gandhi" that the strength and authenticity of Gandhi's nonviolent action drew from its origin in a "metaphysic of man, a philosophical wisdom which is common to Hinduism, Buddhism, Islam, Judaism, and Christianity: that 'truth is the inner law of our being.' "[55] If nonviolence is inseparable from our being, then so are truth and love. Indeed, "Truth is the law of our being," Gandhi observed; and, in another instance, "If love or nonviolence be not the law of our being, the whole of my argument falls to pieces."[56] Merton notes in elaboration that Gandhi's vow of truth ("satyagraha") was a "vow of fidelity to being in all its accessible dimensions";[57] fidelity to "wholeness and being . . . implies a basic respect for life not as a concept . . . but in its deepest, most secret, and most fontal reality."[58]

Amid these central points of commonality between Gandhi's understanding of nonviolence and Merton's understanding of its Christian roots there is a distinguishable difference in emphasis. Whereas Gandhi stresses the inseparability of love, truth, and nonviolence in being, Merton, while hardly in disagreement with this ontological perspective, stresses above all the person, that is, the concrete, sacred, and living reality of each person. Gandhi's view, on the one hand, derives, Merton suggests, from the traditional Vedantist doctrine (in Hinduism) of the Atman ("the true transcendent Self which alone is absolutely real"), while Merton's focus on the person (reflecting his distinction between person and nature in his letter to Dorothy Day) originates in his Christian belief in the indwelling presence of Christ.[59] The significance of this perceptible difference in emphasis does not lie in the different religious beliefs which inform each man's understanding of nonviolence; it may, however, help to illustrate the difference between espousing nonviolence as an ideal and the actual practice of nonviolence as a way of life. Merton's remarks in a letter to James Douglass suggest this latter point. Merton notes that the nonviolent march into the Dharasana salt works led by Gandhi in India on May 21,

1930, in which "wave after wave of marchers" were beaten down, exemplifies the problematical nature of a mass protest in which "the human *personality* of the individual marchers is totally lost."[60] "Without questioning the undoubted heroism of these people, *was* it," Merton asks, "on all their parts a real, fully developed nonviolence? Was it . . . completely and maturely personal, or did they in fact move as a mass?"[61] Merton's underlying points—that nonviolence must be person-oriented and reflect a personal integrity of belief and action—can be applied to dialogue as well.[62]

What are the implications of the philosophy of nonviolence for dialogue? What, in more Mertonian terms, will characterize dialogue oriented to the whole person?

The purpose of nonviolence, Merton notes in "Blessed Are the Meek," is "openness, communication, and dialogue."[63] Fulfillment of this purpose requires first of all that both the adversary and those "whose rights are denied or whose lives are threatened" be regarded equally as persons, as "concrete and living human beings" able to respond wholly to truth and love.[64] Put in simpler terms, one must see the person in the issue and not the issue in the person. When one acts in accordance with nonviolence, one acts for "*the* truth common to [oneself] and to the adversary, *the* right which is objective and universal. [One] is fighting for *everybody*."[65] With "truth" Merton refers "not simply to 'the truth' in a sweeping, idealistic, and purely platonic sense, but to the truth that is incarnate in a concrete human situation."[66]

The nonviolent approach to establishing dialogue precludes selfish motive, physical or psychological manipulation (self-righteousness when used for the attainment of one's own ideal), faith in force or power, or pride in "visible results." It relies rather on humility and "meekness" (implying faith in the transforming power of love and, for the Christian, trust in "the strength of the Lord of truth"), openness and hence a posture of vulnerability, for "only love can attain and preserve the good of all."[67] In nonviolence, love of truth and love of person are inseparable, the integrity of one depending on the integrity of the other. One seeks a common truth, or common good along *with* the other. Nonviolence is an effort at mutual openness and understanding, at mutual openness and responsiveness as persons; "'Person-oriented,' " it "does not seek so much to *control* as to *respond*, and to *awaken response*."[68] "All [nonviolence] seeks," Merton writes, "is the openness of free exchange in which reason and love have freedom of action."[69]

Merton suggests that "openness and simplicity," and respect for the liberty of the other person will be key qualities in building toward mutual openness and responsiveness, in other words, in creating a dynamic in which the capacities for knowing and speaking the truth, and the faculties of speech and voice can be mutually nurtured. In this respect, the capacities for speech and voice can be readily extended to encompass dialogue; dialogue, in fact, can be suggested as an integral part of the development of voice.

"We make ourselves real," to recall Merton's remarks in *No Man Is an Island*, "by telling the truth."[70] By extension, we might also say that "we make both ourselves and others real in our effort to have the truth *mutually* known and spoken." When our effort to speak the truth is joined with the effort to provide another with the opportunity or "space" (implying the alternation, the rhythm of words and silence) to formulate a sincere word (to have and speak from a deep, interior response), then we are recognizing and helping ourselves and others to become real as persons. When this becomes a mutual effort, when we so attend to each other as *persons*, when we allow ourselves to *be* as persons, when we seek to open and awaken response, then we can be said to be united in dialogue and in mutual fidelity to truth. When, conversely, we seek to possess or control the truth, to impose it, or more likely our distorted version of it, then we act as individuals and in the service of our own futile efforts at self-affirmation, at identity through self-assertion, or at self-justification. Discussion becomes struggle, if not competition, the other becomes object, and the mutual deepening or renewal of personal relationship with truth and reality becomes division and separation. We become divided within ourselves as well as between ourselves and, separated from a more loving relationship with others, we are separated from truth.

The quality of our subjective experience as persons, not the force of persuasion or the triumph of an idea, will determine the quality of dialogue; in dialogue, our own growth as whole persons will be intimately bound with the whole experience of others.

COMMUNION

"True communication," Merton reflects in notes entitled "Monastic Experience and East-West Dialogue," "on the deepest level is more than a simple sharing of ideas, of conceptual knowledge, or formulated truth. The kind of communication that is necessary on this deep level must also be 'communion' beyond the level of words, a communion in authentic experience."[71] Merton's remarks are couched in the context of his effort to clarify a contemplative perspective for East-West, inter-monastic dialogue. They reflect his conviction that among contemplatives of "different traditions, disciplines, and religions" who seek the roots of their beliefs in an "ultimate ground" of human experience there is possible a "common ground of verbal understanding." This means more fundamentally a shared existential level of experience—the level "on which [persons] meet beyond their own words and their own understanding in the silence of an ultimate experience which might conceivably not have occurred if they had not met and spoken."[72] Merton suggests further that this "communion" is shared on both a "preverbal" and "postverbal" level; it is in other words implicit in and as important to the "indefinable 'preparation,' 'the predisposition' of mind and heart, necessary for all 'monastic' experience whatever" as in the silent fruits which actual dialogue might yield.[73]

Although aimed at clarifying the deepest possibilities for dialogue and communication among contemplatives within a broadly defined realm of monastic experience, Merton's remarks were motivated by a much larger concern. In attaining to "communion," contemplatives would be serving the vital monastic purpose of witnessing to and evoking the deepest quality of all human experience; to the extent that they realized it, they would make it more real and available to others. "It is the peculiar office of the monk in the modern world," Merton points out, "to keep alive the contemplative experience and to keep the way open for modern technological man to recover the integrity of his own inner depths. . . . Above all, it is important that the element of depth and integrity—this element of inner transcendent freedom—be kept intact as we grow toward the full maturity of . . . universal consciousness."[74] Hence, for Merton, the existential level of communication was at once a broadening, in actuality a *communalizing*, of the general contemplative vocation to greater wholeness and integrity. Such communication was a way to awaken others to a stronger recognition of their own integrity as human beings, accordingly opening them to deeper, fuller human experience and relationship.

Communion is purely experiential and subjective and does not necessarily depend on agreement on specific doctrines or beliefs for its attainment, though it does imply a particular consciousness or predisposition for which the contemplative life especially prepares one. Therefore, Merton's belief in communion as a realizable and desirable experience for contemplatives, and indeed as a universally accessible experience, did not assume a breaking down or imply a disrespect for cultural or religious differences but, rather, significant points of contact within a particular realm of experience that may or may not have been culturally or religiously inspired.[75] In his essay "The Power and Meaning of Love," Merton makes a reference to communion which suggests this point: "A communion of persons implies interiority and depth. It involves the whole being of each person—the mind, the heart, the feelings, the deepest aspiration of the spirit itself. Such union . . . presupposes individual differences—it safeguards the autonomy and character of each as an inviolate and solitary person. . . . Communion means mutual understanding, mutual acceptance, not only in exterior acts to be carried out, but in regard to the inviolate interiority and subjectivity of those who commune with one another."[76] The point to emphasize here is that, far from disregarding difference, Merton's understanding of communion recognizes and in fact embraces difference as part of a more encompassing experience of wholeness.

Insofar as it is "true communication on the deepest level," communion can easily be construed as a natural outgrowth of sincere communication and dialogue; yet, it is presented here as something much more, as an implicit dimension of communication and dialogue, a realization of what is already existentially present or at least believed. In communion, Merton suggests, "we discover an older unity." Speaking to fellow monks, he adds, "My dear brothers, we are already one. But we imagine that we are not. . . . What we have to be is what we are."[77] If dialogue is to be a creative actualization of our relationship as whole persons, then we will be attuned to the dimension of communion which underlies our efforts at communication with another; in this respect, we will recognize the importance of silence to our speech and mutual effort to know and speak the truth.

Genuine communication and dialogue, as suggested in the discussion of speech and voice, and dialogue above, do not simply imply words, or even an exchange of words and ideas, but also, and above all, silence. Our most sincere words emerge from silence and thus presuppose silence, that is, silence understood in a positive way as "presence, awareness, unification, self-discovery."[78] Provided that we listen, this silence will be the true creative source of our speech, in effect making our communication and dialogue complete. Without awareness and attentiveness in silence, our communication and dialogue will not be whole, will not reflect our true creative capacities as whole persons.

As part of his effort to illuminate a basis for ecumenical dialogue within the Christian tradition, Merton wrote, in "THE POORER MEANS: A Meditation on Ways to Unity," of the importance of silence:

> The first of the poorer means to unity is *silence*. While there must be talk, and dialogue, there must also be the silence of those who cannot, or do not, participate in any discussions. This silence is a necessary counterpart of the dialogue, and it must be realized for what it is: an implicit admission that all cannot be said, and that agreements are not perfectly possible, and that all the answers are not within our grasp. Discussion that does not arise out of this silence and depend on it for strength will be illusory.
>
> The silence, even of those who are uneasy, or who do not understand, is therefore a guarantee of wholeness and honesty in our ecumenism.[79]

If our dialogue aims truly to actualize our relationship as whole persons, then we will need to incline our ears to silence, to our own inner integrity, and to the resonances of a deeper presence that signifies our own wholeness and unity as persons. If our dialogue, similarly, is to reflect more than our own narrow viewpoint, then it will have to in all humility be rooted in the silence that embraces not simply us but everybody in the silence in which the unspoken experience of communion can be realized.

As they pertain to the formation of the whole person, communication and dialogue will to some degree reflect the reality, if not the experience of communion. When our communication and dialogue approach this quality, then they will create or renew and deepen community and strengthen our integrity as whole persons. We will be open to creating and responding from our inmost depths as whole persons; we will be able to celebrate our lives together with the confidence and power that come from our enlivened humanity; for, as Merton writes in "The Street Is for Celebration," "Celebration is . . . the creation of a common identity, a common consciousness . . . is everybody making joy . . . is when we let joy make itself out of our love."[80]

Notes

1. See Chapter 4 on "Speaking."
2. Merton, "Cold War Letters," #73, p. 125.
3. Merton, "Symbolism," in *Love and Living*, pp. 48-69; "War and the Crisis of Language," in *The Nonviolent Alternative*, pp. 234-247.
4. Conference Tape #242A, "Mass Communication," May 22, 1966 (Louisville, Ky., Bellarmine College: Thomas Merton Studies Center, unpublished tape); Ferry correspondence in Shannon, ed., *The Hidden Ground of Love*; Ferry was vice-president of the Center for Democratic Institutions at Santa Barbara at the time and provided Merton with information relevant to contemporary issues.
5. Merton, *Conjectures*, p. 236.
6. Ibid.
7. Ibid., pp. 237, 238.
8. Ibid.
9. Ibid., p. 240.
10. Conference Tape #242A, "Mass Communication."
11. Ibid.
12. Ibid.

13. Ibid.

14. Conference Tape #242B, "Description of Vietnamese Monk's Visit," May 29, 1966 (Louisville, Ky.: Bellarmine College: Thomas Merton Studies Center, unpublished tape).

15. Ibid.

16. Ibid.

17. Merton, "Nhat Hanh Is My Brother," in *Nonviolent Alternative*, pp. 263-264.

18. Merton, *Vow of Conversation*, p. 187.

19. Merton, "World," in *Love and Living*, p. 106.

20. Merton, "Symbolism," in *Love and Living*, p. 56.

21. Ibid., p. 52.

22. Ibid., p. 53.

23. Ibid.

24. Ibid.

25. Ibid., p. 60.

26. Ibid., pp. 48, 57.

27. Ibid., p. 60.

28. Ibid., p. 54.

29. See, for example, Merton, " 'Baptism in the Forest': Wisdom and Initiation in William Faulkner," in Hart, ed., *Literary Essays*, pp. 92-116, and "Poetry and Contemplation: A Reappraisal," in *Literary Essays*, pp. 338-354.

30. Merton, " 'Baptism in the Forest,' " in Hart, ed., *Literary Essays*, p. 99.

31. Ibid., 98; In "Poetry and Contemplation: A Reappraisal," written almost ten years earlier, Merton employs "contemplative" similarly; it seems that he adopted "sapiential" as a more inclusive term in the interim.

32. Ibid., p. 99.

33. Ibid., pp. 99-100.

34. Ibid., p. 100.

35. Merton, "The Need for a New Education," in *Contemplation in a World of Action*, p. 207. This article addresses the question of monastic education in the context of modern society; I would submit that most of its ideas are relevant to the broader discussion of Merton's ideas on education contained in these pages. Cf., Conference Tape #306B, "Monastic Education," September 9, 1968 (Louisville, Ky.: Bellarmine College: Thomas Merton Studies Center, unpublished tape).

36. Merton, "War and the Crisis of Language," in *The Nonviolent Alternative*, p. 240.

37. Merton to Wilbur Ferry, April 11, 1967, in Shannon, ed., *The Hidden Ground of Love*, p. 232; Merton, "War and the Crisis of Language," in *The Nonviolent Alternative*.

38. Merton, "War and the Crisis of Language," in *The Nonviolent Alternative*, p. 238.

39. Ibid., p. 237.

40. Ibid., pp. 237-238. Merton wrote in a similar vein to Jacques Maritain, "Advertising is one of the great *loci classici* for the theology of the devil"; Merton to Jacques Maritain, June 11, 1963 (Louisville, Ky., Bellarmine College: Thomas Merton Studies Center, unpublished correspondence).

41. Ibid., p. 240.

42. Ibid., p. 241.

43. Conference Tape #4B, "Solitude, Community and Poverty," *Mystic Life Series* (Chappaqua, N.Y.: Electronic-Paperbacks, 1976).

44. Merton, *No Man*, p. xv.

45. Merton to Dorothy Day, in *Seeds*, pp. 253-259; "Blessed Are the Meek," in *The Nonviolent Alternative*, pp. 208-218.

46. Merton to Dorothy Day, *Seeds*, p. 254.

47. Ibid.

48. Ibid., p. 255.

49. Ibid.

50. Merton, "A Tribute to Gandhi," in *The Nonviolent Alternative*, pp. 178-184; "Gandhi and the One-Eyed Giant," in *Gandhi on Nonviolence*, p. 20.

51. Merton, *Gandhi*, p. 25.

52. Merton, "Blessed Are the Meek," in *The Nonviolent Alternative*, p. 209.

53. Merton, *Gandhi*, p. 24.

54. Martin Luther King Jr., *Stride Toward Freedom* (San Francisco: Harper & Row, 1958), p. 106.

55. Merton, "A Tribute to Gandhi," in *The Nonviolent Alternative*, pp. 182-183.

56. Merton, *Gandhi*, pp. 11, 25.

57. Merton, "A Tribute to Gandhi," in *The Nonviolent Alternative*, p. 183.

58. Ibid.

59. See "Blessed Are the Meek," in *The Nonviolent Alternative*, pp. 209, 216.

60. Merton to James Douglass, April 17, 1967, in Shannon, ed., *The Hidden Ground Of Love*, p. 165.

61. Ibid.; Cf., "Blessed Are the Meek," in *The Nonviolent Alternative*, p. 211.

62. See Merton, "Blessed Are the Meek," in *The Nonviolent Alternative*, p. 217.

63. Ibid., p. 211.

64. Ibid.

65. Ibid., p. 209.

66. Ibid., p. 211.

67. Ibid., p. 213.

68. Ibid., p. 217.

69. Ibid. In unpublished notes entitled "The Basis of Christian Nonviolence" (Louisville, Ky.: Bellarmine College: The Thomas Merton Studies Center), Merton writes, "The true power of nonviolence lies in the fact that it does not seek to gain advantage over others by manipulating the forces of human nature, but that it appeals directly to the person, seeking not control but response as the starting point for concerned dialog."

70. Merton, *No Man*, p. 188.

71. Merton, "Monastic Experience and East-West Dialogue," Appendix IV, in *Asian Journal*, p. 315.

72. Ibid.

73. Ibid.

74. Ibid., p. 317.

75. Ibid., p. 312.

76. Merton, "The Power and Meaning of Love," in *Disputed Questions*, pp. 118-119.

77. Merton, "Thomas Merton's View of Monasticism," Appendix III, in *Asian Journal*, p. 308.

78. Merton, "Creative Silence," in *Love and Living*, p. 35.

79. Merton, "THE POORER MEANS: A Meditation on Ways to Unity," *Sobornost* (Winter-Spring, 1966), p. 77; see also "Ecumenism and Renewal," in *Contemplation in a World of Action*, p. 196.

80. Merton, "The Street Is for Celebration," in *Love and Living*, p. 47.

7

Teaching and the Education Of the Whole Person

In education defined as the formation of the whole person and in which learning is meant ultimately to dispose the person for discovery of the whole self, in what might teaching, or quality of teaching, consist? What understandings will orient and guide one's approach in the teaching-learning process? These are natural questions to pose as part of a concluding effort to suggest the significance of Merton's ideas, beliefs, and example for education, and it is the primary purpose of this chapter to address them. The intent in addressing them, however, is not to provide definitive answers or to suggest that they can be provided in the space of a chapter. It is rather to confirm the validity and importance of these questions in the context of a discussion of Merton's ideas, hence to establish that Merton's view of education (and thus education understood from a spiritual perspective) has a clear and compelling and concrete analogy in teaching.

Merton's descriptions of teachers he admired and his sense of the significance of his own efforts as a teacher provide excellent starting points from which to build an understanding of teaching in relation to the formation of the whole person. It is important to emphasize, however, that these pedagogical sketches suggest personal characteristics of teachers and teaching in accord with Merton's belief regarding education rather than a method or technique. These characteristics can be considered general landmarks in the broad landscape of teaching. For the teacher practitioner who adopts the questions above as his or her own, they may serve as guideposts in exploring a personal sense of purpose, direction, and participation in the process of education.

MENTORS AND MODELS

Though infrequent in his writing, Merton's personal reflections on several of his own teachers and on the nature and impact of their teaching provide a vivid portrait of pedagogy which exemplifies education aimed at the formation of the whole person. Three teachers are prominent in this respect and were specifically mentioned by Merton in his written response to Mary Declan Martin's request (noted in Chapter 2) for "some information on your life and most importantly your views on education."[1] Two of the teachers, Mark Van Doren (literature) and Dan Walsh (philosophy), were professors of Merton's during his undergraduate and graduate years at Columbia University with whom he developed close, lifelong friendships. The third was "M. Delmas," Merton's French language teacher when he was twelve years old in the Lycée Ingres in France. Merton remarks on the exemplary qualities of Van Doren and Walsh in *The Seven Storey Mountain* and on M. Delmas in "On Remembering M. Delmas," a tribute he wrote in retrospect for Morris Ernst's anthology, *The Teacher* (1967).[2]

Merton introduces Mark Van Doren in *The Seven Storey Mountain* in the midst of recounting his undergraduate experiences while at Columbia (having previously spent an undistinguished year at Cambridge University in England) and explaining their significance for his intellectual and spiritual growth. Van Doren assumes an almost figurative stature in Merton's narrative. The simple integrity with which he taught—his genuineness, the honesty and directness of his approach—struck Merton profoundly. The humility and sincerity reflected in Van Doren's teaching contrasted the airy pretense that characterized much of the teaching Merton observed during his previous university-level experience, especially at Cambridge University. Merton began to take longer strides down the path of self-understanding under the influence of Van Doren's example, more readily searching for, recognizing, and confronting what was shallow or insincere in his own thinking.[3] How, as seen through Merton's eyes, did Van Doren's teaching manifest his personal qualities of honesty, forthrightness, and unpretentiousness? In what other ways was Merton as a student affected?

Van Doren's unmediated love for literature compelled Merton's attention. For Van Doren, the study of literature did not depend on the critical perspectives of other disciplines, such as economics or psychology, in order to be valid or revealing. "Literature was treated . . . simply as literature."[4] This approach maintained the inherent value of literature itself as a mode of human expression through which something vital of fundamental human experience (Merton mentions "life, death, time, love, sorrow, fear" as examples) could be uniquely communicated.[5] Yet it is Van Doren's "manner of approach," his unbiased treatment, more than the worth of literature that it affirms, which leaves the strongest imprint on Merton.

In "his manner of dealing with his subject with perfect honesty and objectivity and without evasions," Van Doren encouraged in Merton a deeper, more personal (in contrast to a doctrinal or otherwise preconceived) and wholly honest response to literature.[6] Van Doren's ingenuous "manner of approach" encouraged students to likewise approach, understand, learn from, and judge literature as it was, to engage it directly as an evocative symbolic expression of human experience. Van Doren in this respect "purified and educated the perceptions of his students." He accomplished this process through the study of literature "by teaching [his students] how to read a book and how to tell a good book from a bad, genuine writing from falsity and pastiche."[7] Essentially, Van Doren provided his students with an experience of their personal capacity for honest perception and unpretentious thought—that is, thought which, intellectually speaking, did not depend first and foremost on its conformity to the ideas, precepts, expectations, or theories of others.

"Knowledge," then, was not so much *received* in Van Doren's classroom as *conceived*; it was deeply personal and original in that it was formulated uniquely by each person. Van Doren's teaching can be said to have been person-oriented or personalistic in that it allowed this original formulation to take place.[8]

There is no doubt that the process of sincere and honest thinking fostered by Van Doren had a vital educational importance for Merton. Particularly in the aftermath of World War II and the revelation of how so many otherwise "sane" and rational citizens complied with morally vacuous Nazi thinking, he was acutely aware of the susceptibility of the human mind to subversion. Thus the virtue in Van Doren's teaching that he highlights in *The Seven Storey Mountain* becomes for him a larger social imperative. In his essay "Christianity and Totalitarianism," for example, he points out that we must nurture love first of all by safeguarding "the liberty and integrity of the human person." "We must provide an education that strengthens [us] against the noise, the violence, and the half-truths of our materialistic society," he declares.[9] This is clearly the quality of education that he felt Van Doren's teaching exemplified.

According to Merton, Van Doren elicited honesty and depth of thought from his students through his questioning as well as his manner. He recalls that Van Doren's questions "were very good and if you tried to answer them intelligently, you found yourself saying excellent things that you did not know you knew, and that you had not, in fact, known before. He had 'educed' them from you by his question. His classes were literally 'education'—they brought things out of you, they made your mind produce its own explicit ideas."[10] In evoking such honesty and depth of thought, Van Doren's questions made it possible for his students to have an experience that at once brought them into a more authentic contact with literature and themselves. The significance of the "excellent things" that were said lay as much in their interior origin and the personal experience of knowing thus affirmed as in their content. The one experience was attendant on the other; together they reflected a more integrated experience of self, intellect, and voice.

Van Doren's teaching disposed his students to appreciate authenticity in the realm of intellectual endeavor in general and in their very manner of regarding the world. At least this was Merton's experience. To Van Doren's clear-mindedness, his focus on the essential, his looking "directly for the quiddities of things," Merton attributes much of his own later receptivity to "the good seed of scholastic philosophy."[11] Merton here implies his openness and attentiveness to that which was substantial, true, and real. Merton might say that his experience as a student in Van Doren's class disposed him to a deeper consciousness of himself as a whole person.

In one of his last conferences at Gethsemani before his fatal trip to Asia, on "Monastic Education" (September 17, 1968), Merton noted that "education should be something broad and deep . . . a consistent broadening and deepening process to give us not only knowledge but also wisdom; it should be an opening up and a developing of the human capacities of each one of us."[12] Though couched in his reflections on monastic education, Merton's comments have a much more general resonance, which his experience as a student under Mark Van Doren to some extent exemplifies.

From the quality of Merton's "educational" experience with Mark Van Doren it is not difficult to draw a connection to the human capacity to know, understand, and communicate the truth integral to the development of the voice of the whole person. The originality, depth, and authenticity of Merton's experience (Van Doren's questions "brought things out of you, they made your mind produce its own explicit ideas") made it more than an intellectual exercise. The habitude of honest and unpretentious thought cultivated by Van Doren deepened Merton's respect for authenticity in himself and in his perception of his world. It served in effect to affirm and enhance his ability to relate to the world more fully as a whole person.

Van Doren was an example of a "sapiential" (denoting wisdom) teacher for Merton.[13] He makes this designation while discussing the sapiential quality of William Faulkner's literary symbolism in an essay written many years after his account of Van Doren's teaching in *The Seven Storey Mountain*.[14] Linking this reference to Van Doren with the earlier account, one can readily infer that Merton is thinking especially of Van Doren's ability to engage his students in considering the deepest symbolic levels of literary communication ("directed . . . at . . . man's own understanding of himself"[15]). Through his questioning and his insight, Van Doren was able to open his students to what Merton describes in reference to Faulkner as the power of literary symbols to "bring you into living participation with an experience of basic and universal human values which words can *point* to but cannot fully attain."[16] In providing the opportunity for this quality of personal experience through the study of literature, Van Doren clearly exemplifies a full measure of person-oriented teaching. The learning as well as the teaching can be considered sapiential, oriented to fulfilling what Merton asserted in "Learning to Live" should be "the purpose of all learning"—"to dispose [one] for . . . [self-discovery]."[17] Van Doren's teaching in this respect helps exemplify education as "an opening up and a developing of the human capacities of each one of us," and, moreover, "a broadening and deepening process" which gives us "not only knowledge, but also wisdom." Elsewhere, Merton indicates the value in the modern world of studying philosophy, anthropology, comparative religion, and psychology, in addition to the humanities, in order to broaden and deepen sapiential awareness.[18] Certainly this point deserves further study as part of the effort to understand education which would bear on the formation of the whole person.

Several general but familiar themes vis-à-vis the formation of the whole person resound, then, in Merton's account of Van Doren's teaching. Van Doren's intellectual honesty and his humble and unprejudiced approach to studying literature (without reading into it "some favorite private doctrine") prefigure Merton's own rigorous avoidance of frames of reference which he believed might delimit his apprehension of reality or predetermine his own perceptions. Similarly, Van Doren's efforts at "educing" his students' "own explicit ideas," and "purifying and educating their perceptions," suggest the interior integrity which characterizes the discipline of speaking, the development of voice, and an authentic personal quality of communication. Finally, by helping his students to distinguish the "good" from the "bad" in a book, and the "genuine" from the false in writing, Van Doren, in Merton's experience, sharpened their inclination and ability to perceive what was real, true, and substantial. Essentially, Van Doren's teaching of literature provided experiences which fostered not only Merton's intellectual growth but also—inasmuch as they implied attention to the origin of perceptions and perspectives, the innate capacity to speak the truth, and a more integrated, whole sense of self—the formation of the whole person. It is in this respect that he had a person-oriented pedagogy.

The personalistic quality of Mark Van Doren's teaching can be elaborated with reference to other aspects of the formation of the whole person and broadened to encompass teaching outside the realm of literature. The importance of the character, bearing, and example of the teacher, however, must be emphasized first.

What distinguishes Mark Van Doren and also Dan Walsh and M. Delmas as teachers are the personal qualities of humility, honesty, and simplicity that they clearly have in common according to Merton's portraits. As noted above, Mark Van Doren dealt with his subject "with perfect honesty and objectivity and without evasions." Dan Walsh, with "smiling simplicity," "used to efface himself entirely in the solid and powerful mind of St. Thomas [Aquinas]."[19] M. Delmas "was a small, discreet, unassuming, unobtrusive, smiling type . . . [whom] I fully believed . . . never said anything he did not mean."[20] These qualities by themselves were admirable, yet by themselves could not have awakened the particular attention Merton gave to them, nor have molded the keen intelligence and approach to teaching exemplified by the men who had them. They communicated and reflected a deeper origin, as revealed especially in Merton's essay on M. Delmas.

"I think he had the same sort of quality," Merton writes of M. Delmas, "I have always appreciated in all the teachers who have given me something really important. (I have written elsewhere of many of these, such as Mark Van Doren and Dan Walsh.) M. Delmas had a certain tact, a humility in the presence of life and reality."[21] Humility on the part of these teachers, then, was a form of witness to life; life itself, it might be said, provided a noticeable proportion and perspective to their teaching, helping them to focus attention on what was essential and real, and on the person. Thus their teaching, especially as reflected in their "manner of approach," was devoid of intellectual pretense, personal affectation, or artifice. They didn't acquire credibility through "official" or "authoritative" pronouncements, through the exercise of formal authority, or, it may be readily inferred, through a manipulation of specialized knowledge. They simply did not pretend to know or teach more than they knew, any more than they expected anything but honest and sincere effort from their students. As Merton says of M. Delmas, "He liked what he thought. He did not despise students as such. He took an interest in other human beings. He found human beings more important than regulations, theories, programs, systems, and collective prescriptions. Briefly, he was a simple, honest, perhaps flexible human being who did not insist on being taken for anything other than what he was: A man interested in helping young people use the French language with a certain amount of intelligence."[22]

As a consequence of his humility before life, his clear sense of purpose, and his honest demeanor, M. Delmas, in Merton's estimation, understood that "the teacher exists for the student, not the other way around."[23] M. Delmas, for one, was therefore "patient," expecting not "great results," but "some degree of thought." He "simply maintained an atmosphere" in which boys of twelve could receive the "light" and "gift" of understanding (beyond knowing, that is, simply what was "correct").[24]

Merton draws special attention to M. Delmas's patience, citing it in connection with a particular moment of understanding that he enjoyed ("He helped me discover that grammar was for men, not men for grammar."[25]), and contrasting it to one of his more general concerns—the desire and press for results. By extension, Merton's discussion of M. Delmas' patience suggests in general the importance of an orientation toward "formation" rather than "results" in person-oriented teaching. This conclusion draws strong support from the concept of "personal" knowledge introduced earlier in this chapter and from the understanding of time, speaking, voice, and dialogue developed in previous chapters.

Just as "the hope for results" harbored by those engaged in social action can distort perspective and divert attention from the essential person-oriented nature of one's work, it can subvert the quality of teaching implicated by "the formation of the whole person." To recall Merton's letter to James Forest (Chapter 5), one may hope for "results," but not depend on them, concentrating instead on "the value, the truth of the work itself."[26] Applied to teaching, Merton's perspective suggests a person-oriented approach commensurate with the qualities and capacities of the whole person.

In education defined as the formation of the whole person, teaching will not in general be governed by a paradigm of "means" and "ends" in which the "ends" represent a predetermined result and the "means" a program for achieving it. This approach, while it may readily serve in instances pertaining to specific bodies of knowledge or skills, does not embrace the whole person. It focuses teaching on an objective end. The person *qua* student becomes an object, too, ultimately reinforcing a view of the world as the functional interrelation of objects.

The person, however, is subject. A person-oriented approach to teaching, as in the case of Mark Van Doren, will thus attend to the subjective quality of personal experience. It is the quality of personal experience, as distinct from the treatment of learning as an accumulation of facts or the acquisition of skills (though not excluding these), or as a link to an imagined future, competitive "success," that will help form the person's capacity to see, hear, speak, think honestly, and relate more wholly to reality and others.

SILENCE AND ATTENTIVENESS AS MODES OF LEARNING

In group discussion (implying dialogue), the quality of personal experience will be determined by the extent to which participants are encouraged to speak the words which express their deepest authentic understanding of the reality or truth that they perceive. Questions which elicit the honest, explicit ideas of participants, as exemplified in Mark Van Doren's classroom, constitute one important form of encouragement. But the dialogic process will also be enhanced by participants' careful attention to the interior origin of their own words. "Space," or silence, openness and attentiveness, will be important to the effort to discern and formulate in words one's deepest response to vital questions, and thus to the development of the personal capacities for speech and dialogue.

Parker Palmer, educator and writer, has explored the relationship between silence and speech in teaching in his book, *To Know as We Are Known: A Spirituality of Education*.[27] His work strongly supports the interpretation of Merton's ideas and their exemplification in teaching presented here.

Palmer contends that silence is as important to discussion as speech, in effect creating a space in which greater clarity of thought can crystallize. Palmer relates that he alternates times for quiet reflection with times for speaking in his teaching. He counsels, however, that "silence must be introduced cautiously; we must allow ourselves to be slowly re-formed in its discipline before it can become an effective teaching tool . . . [and] potent space for learning."[28]

Palmer suggests that the experience of silence provides students with the opportunity for personal and collective recollection, thus with an important "space" in which to realize and formulate in words more clearly what they most sincerely mean. He doesn't, however, present the use of silence merely as a functional teaching tool. Palmer clearly believes that silence itself can transform a collective experience into a communal one. When alternated with verbal communication, silence can renew a group in the common experience of a reality beneath words, in a sense of unity or common relationship. He explains, "Eventually my students feel a sense of community in the silence that is deeper than what they feel when the words are flowing fast and hard. . . . In the silence we are more likely to sense the unity of truth which lies beneath our overanalyzed world, the relatedness between us and others and the world we inhabit and study. When we emerge from silence with this sense of unity in our hearts, it is easier to speak and hear words of troth [by which Palmer means the words through which one expresses one's essential relationship to reality]."[29] Palmer not only recognizes the close affinity of words and silence discussed earlier in the sections on speaking and dialogue but also what was for Merton "the deepest form of communication"—"communion." When communication on this level has been experienced, then the formation of the whole person has indeed been served. One has not only experienced a personalized knowledge but the deeper relationship to others in which our unity as persons in the "hidden wholeness" and love of God is intimated.

Just as silence is integral to speech, then, it can also be considered as an integral part of group discussion and experience. Particularly for the teacher, this realization implies not only the importance of providing "space" for the clear and honest personal formulation of thoughts and words but of recognizing that the words that are spoken may not fully reflect what is sincerely intended, intuited, or understood. Therefore, instead of concentrating solely on the words spoken, or on evaluating response, the teacher (and/or fellow members of a discussion group), through careful questioning and the provision of a silent "space," might respectfully provide the opportunity for a clearer formulation of words and more integrated expression of voice to occur. The teacher would in this way be attending as much to the personal, interior experience of knowing underlying the creative generation of speech as to the actual words presented (for those without the capacity for speaking or writing, other forms of creative expression might be encouraged). Thus the teacher would be acting in support of the whole person. Again, the intent in these instances would not be to contrive a situation aimed at obtaining a predetermined, "visible" result but simply to attend to "formation," to provide the space for an integrated experience of self and voice, for a more wholly personal experience of knowing, for a clear apprehension and expression of the realities within one's personal focus. In terms of the formation of the whole person, it is the opportunity for this quality of personal experience which will be most important.

Parker Palmer suggests that silence is a "discipline," hence, provision for quiet time in the context of discussion or other group activity in itself clearly will not ensure that a full experience and expression of the whole person will take place. In order for "quiet" to become an experience of silence and personal recollection, if not of deeper unity, one cannot remain inert or passive, for the discipline of silence implies as well a discipline of openness and attentiveness.

The discussion in Chapter 4 established that cultivation of the faculties of seeing, hearing, and speaking will depend on a discipline of openness and attentiveness. This discipline can be viewed as equally vital to the formation of the intellectual and spiritual life of the whole person. As indicated in Chapter 4, learning to be attentive entails a vulnerable and open readiness to receive beyond one's own self-defined and asserted limits. Attentiveness requires a humble, yet passionate desire to know and become more present to truth and reality beyond prejudicial interior habits of thought and action.

A key aspect of the discipline of openness and attentiveness involves disposing one's whole self as much as possible to receive—as it pertains to things, to receive a clearer understanding of their reality; as it pertains to people, a deeper recognition of, love for, and identification with them as unique persons; as it pertains to both people and things in unique situations, a deeper understanding of truth and awareness of God's presence. Disposing oneself to receive implies as well a "letting go" of "the false drive for self-affirmation" or the will to self-assertion, both of which tend to place one over and against rather than in a more whole relationship with reality and people.

Insofar as it implies a "letting go" and the readiness to receive something fundamentally new, the experience of openness involves some degree of vulnerability. In openness, one leaves the sanctuary of the known to risk contact with the unknown. One becomes willing to relinquish or refashion an old perception or assumption in the face of a new perspective. One even becomes willing to live with the unsettling feelings of confusion, puzzlement, and uncertainty that can accompany the prospect of a change in self-understanding, knowledge of the world, or relationship. Openness need not, however, be a fearful experience. In an atmosphere of patience and support, openness and its implicit promise of a deeper or renewed sense of self and reality, or what Merton might say is an inherent yearning for truth, can be sustained. In group silence, for example, openness can become an experience of solidarity and heighten the desire to know and become receptive to the truth. Hence, undergirding the student's effort to discover and express what is in his or her deepest grasp will be the teacher's (and/or fellow students') acceptance, patience, and understanding; in a word, love.

In notes that he prepared as handouts for his monastic classes at Gethsemani, Merton stresses that quality and depth of intellectual formation will require the ability to collect oneself and focus one's mental activity, that is, to give attention. According to Merton, "attention" is "a concentration of conscious mental activity upon selected matter of thought or desire, other thoughts and desires being excluded."[30] As he acknowledges in his notes, this is a complex psychological act, requiring not only "inhibition of thoughts that are not desired," but the "coordinated activity of memory, imagination, power of association, intelligence, [and] will."[31] Yet it is a discipline one can work toward, in concert with the development of openness, honest perception and thought, patience and other aspects of the formation of the whole person fostered through silence, questioning, careful communication, and related aspects of teaching.

The capacity for attention was important to Merton's own ongoing study and writing. Amid a rigorous monastic work schedule and discipline of prayer, time for personal study was limited. Even while living at the hermitage, when his communal responsibilities were few, Merton's typical day, by his own account, allowed for about two hours each of reading and writing (interspersed with manual work, periods of meditation and prayer, and walks in the surrounding hills).[32] Yet, as his many reading notebooks and prodigious writing output indicate, the times he set aside for study and writing were fruitful.[33] Matthew Kelty, a former novice under Merton, has observed, "He was always totally immersed in whatever he was doing and never played idly at something which was serious. . . . He made very good use of his time."[34]

Merton's sheer productivity is deceptive, however, suggesting that bulk, not quality, resulted from the "good use" of his limited time. While it is true that he was often pressed to complete promised work, quality, not quantity of effort was most important to him.[35] He did not value attentiveness simply because it enabled him to get more work done. For Merton, attentiveness was intimately connected to a deeper, more integrated inner experience, understood in serious reflection, meditation, and prayer. As he explained to his Pakistani friend, Sufi scholar Abdul Aziz: "There are times when it is necessary to read, and even to read quite a lot, in order to store up material and get new perspectives. In the solitary life . . . moderate reading is . . . normal. Provided that more time is spent in prayer and meditation than in reading."[36]

Inasmuch as attentiveness implies depth, not necessarily breadth of effort, cultivating the capacity for attentiveness will depend less on covering a particular range of material than on the depth and quality of each engagement. Consistent with this idea, Merton provides in his mimeographed notes on intellectual development selective examples of questions or statements (as befitting his purpose, dealing with the spiritual life and spiritual reading) that his students might quietly focus on, suggesting that openness, patience, and steadiness will support a concentrated mental effort.[37]

Particularly in intellectual endeavor, the capacity for attentiveness will clearly have a greater priority in the formation of the whole person than the simple aim for and achievement of results. In the context of teaching and learning, the emphasis will be less on showing what one knows, on self-assertion or domination (effort originating more in the ego and will), than on collecting oneself (an effort of the whole person) so that one can become more open to knowing or apprehending an essential truth or objective reality in its wholeness.

While Merton clearly links the capacity for attentiveness to intellectual growth, he emphasizes that it is a discipline affecting the whole life of the person. Learning to become attentive is tantamount to learning to become as awake and alive, and as open and present to life—ultimately to God—as possible. In terms of intellectual activity (whether involving reading, writing, speaking, formulating words, studying a natural phenomenon, etc.), this means opening oneself wholly to a greater knowledge of, and ultimately a more concrete, intimate relationship with reality and truth. As it pertains to seeing, hearing, and speaking, a capacity for attentiveness will enable one to look for, listen to, and apprehend more fully the wondrous and singular reality of an object. In the realm of contemplative prayer, the discipline of attentiveness will enable one who loves and desires to know God to become more open to God's presence.[38]

Like Merton, Simone Weil, the twentieth century philosopher, social activist, and spiritual writer introduced earlier (see Chapter 3), linked the capacity for attentiveness to the ability to know the truth and considered it essential for prayer. Comparable to Merton's emphasis on patience and humility, Weil disassociates attention from pride, suggesting that attention is not so much an act of will as a manifestation of the love of truth and the desire to learn. More emphatically than Merton, she states the importance of attentiveness to all forms of study, going so far as to maintain that quality in learning should be judged by the quality of attentiveness one has during the learning process. As she explains it, "The authentic and pure values—truth, beauty, and goodness—in the activity of a human being are the result of one and the same act, a certain application of the full attention to the object. Teaching should have no aim but to prepare, by training the attention, for the possibility of such an act."[39] In relating the value in human activity to attentiveness, Weil suggests that a certain quality of creative personal response is made possible through attention. "Extreme attention," she writes, "is what constitutes the creative faculty in man."[40]

The extent to which Simone Weil's understanding of the nature and significance of attentiveness correlates with Merton's accentuates its importance to the formation of the whole person. In the realm of teaching and learning, an emphasis on attentiveness will enhance the personal and mutual effort to attain greater clarity and understanding of truth or clearer focus on the realities comprehensible in a particular context. And just as it will demand a full effort at openness on the part of the whole person, attentiveness will encourage a more whole, personal, and creative response in those instances when a new understanding is acquired.

MERTON'S EXAMPLE AS LEARNER AND TEACHER

Certainly Merton's poetry, photography, and calligraphies ("signs") represent his effort as a whole person to respond creatively to what, in openness and attentiveness, he saw, heard, and apprehended. Merton's monastic experience clearly nourished this dialectic of openness and creative response to life. One has only to read "The Fire Watch," the prose piece which concludes his first Gethsemani journal, *The Sign of Jonas*, or *Hagia Sophia*, for rich examples of this dialectic at work. During the period of the late sixties, in the midst of his efforts to respond to social questions involving race and peace, Merton found much joy in working on his long poem, *The Geography of Lograire*. He also conceived and edited four issues of an informal, mimeographed (at the monastery) magazine dubbed *Monks Pond* during this period. As he explained to his friend Wilbur Ferry, he solicited for this "little magazine" "poetry, creative stuff, Asian relig. texts, or other unusual material (Hasidic stories, etc.)." It was precisely the "unusual," in the sense of an authentic response to life out of the conventional social mainstream, that interested Merton in this effort. He wrote excitedly to Ferry of the prospective first issue, "Already have some fine poetry from good people. It's grooving."[41]

One can certainly encourage a creative response to life through teaching as part of a dialectic involving openness and attentiveness. Merton's personal encouragement and guidance of others through his correspondence, involving in particular mature poets and writers, and most especially young aspiring ones, is in this respect illustrative.[42] To Laura Knight, for example, who sent Merton a poem along with her request for a list of those of his books he would recommend she read for her term paper on him as a twentieth-century American writer, Merton responded in part, "I wish you lots of luck with your thesis. I liked your poem. It is good to think about deep things; keep that up."[43] In a more detailed and ongoing correspondence, Merton encouraged the poetic efforts of Nancy Fly Bredenberg, a student at Vassar College at the time, indicating also that some of her work might find its way into his lively journal of offbeat poetry and writing, *Monks Pond*. "Don't be shy, send me some of your poems too," he wrote in February of 1968, adding, "If I don't use them—well all I can do is send them back and that happens to everyone all the time."[44] Bredenberg subsequently sent Merton one of her poems (with her self-criticism) and not surprisingly elicited a critical, but kind and supportive response: "The idea is lovely and I do want the idea very much for the magazine. The form is wrong . . . with condensation . . . certainly it will be beautiful."[45]

From June of 1967 through her high school graduation in 1968, Merton engaged in a warm and charming correspondence initiated by a young Californian, Suzanne Butorovich. Upon reading of her plans to publish an underground newspaper ("The Clique Courier"), Merton responded enthusiastically, "I like underground movements and publications, they are irresistable"; and, in the spirit of his own *Monks Pond*, he submitted some of his recent work (apparently from *Cables to the Ace*) for editorial consideration ("Maybe you won't like any but if you listen to it right you probably will").[46] He concluded another letter with, "Lots of love. I look forward with confident joy to the next number of CC."[47] When plans for the projected publication appeared to stagnate, Merton gently chided his young friend, "When is Clique C. coming out? It rules yr. life; better rule *it*."[48]

Merton's correspondence with Suzanne was mutually enriching in a way that clearly went beyond his encouragement of her creative personal expression. Merton invited her to "educate" him in "pop music." She obligingly sent the "Hippy Hermit" words to several Beatles tunes with other information about the group. "I really like the Beatles and their ideas and their ways of doing and saying things," Merton responded. "I think they are absolutely all right and make sense."[49] In reply to one of her questions, Merton sent an annotated list of suggested readings on Zen by D. T. Suzuki.[50] And in what would prove to be his last letter to Suzanne (June 4, 1968), Merton ends with an exhortation: "I was very happy to get your graduation picture. You have grown into a very charming and interesting young woman. . . . Go forth into the wide world and help it, if possible, make some kind of sense. Or anyway less nonsense."[51]

One of the important characteristics of the Bredenberg and Butorovich correspondences, in addition to the special friendship each nurtured and Merton's encouragement of their personal creativity, was the degree of openness, of open response and open exchange, that each fostered. This was characteristic of so many of Merton's epistolary relationships. He established through his correspondence a vital interpersonal network for the encouragement, exchange, and critical appraisal of writing, books, and ideas in a variety of areas, including principally religion and literature.[52] Letter writing enabled him to explore and support the exploration of the genuine and personal in himself and others. Essentially, Merton's correspondence was a form of his participation in creative dialogue.

"The one thing that most blocks [openness] is getting oneself permanently identified and so to speak classified as the holder of one or other set opinion," Merton wrote in commenting on Cold War attitudes to Wilbur Ferry. "We have got to keep thinking and asking questions," he added.[53] Merton's correspondence was instrumental in allowing him to do precisely that—to clarify his thought and widen his perspectives in numerous areas and on a myriad of questions. Particular examples of this impact of his correspondence abound. To cite but a few: Michael Mott, Merton biographer, illustrates how Merton's interchange with the writer Czeslaw Milosz helped him to become more aware of a subtle type of activism or nonviolence which could deepen division not only between but also within those on either side of a question, thus limiting the very openness sought;[54] in corresponding with (and occasionally meeting with) Wilbur "Ping" Ferry, vice-president of the Center for Democratic Institutions at the time, Merton acquired information related to various social issues, including especially mass communication; Merton's exchange with the Zen scholar Daisetz T. Suzuki, published in part in *Zen and the Birds of Appetite*, exemplified the possibilities for East-West religious dialogue.[55]

Merton's correspondence added a vital personal dimension to

his study. Whether scholars, poets, religious leaders, students, draft resisters, peace activists, or artists, his correspondents lent a wealth of personal experience to his intellectual understanding and compassionate identification with others. In some cases, this influence was extended to his immediate community at Gethsemani, where Merton during his hermitage years offered weekly conferences on topics ranging from Blake and Faulkner to Sufism and native "Cargo" movements in the South Pacific and introduced speakers such as Dan Walsh and Thich Nhat Hanh, the Buddhist monk of Vietnam who inspired Merton's "Nhat Hanh Is My Brother."[56]

The quality and extent of Merton's personal correspondence is yet another indication of his effort to create and sustain openness and attentiveness and to question and widen basic perspectives as a condition for growth as a whole person. Essentially, his correspondence ensured his continuous engagement in a personal dialogue with others, particularly with members of the intellectual community. In this respect, Merton's correspondence points once again to the nature and importance of dialogue to a teaching-learning process oriented to the formation of the whole person.

Reflecting on the conference on "The Spiritual Roots of Protest" held with peace activists at Gethsemani in 1964, Merton felt that openness enabled members to get "in contact with reality and truth in a way that is not met with everyday."[57] As perceived by Merton, that experience can be considered an indication of what is possible on a broader scale in the realm of education. The disciplines of openness and attentiveness and efforts at thoughtful, honest, personal response—whether fostered through a balance of questioning and silence, through support of the effort to formulate a sincere word, through an effort to determine and focus on the essential and factual, or through the willingness to "let go" of preconceptions—can mold participation in group discussion. Such a faithful approach can help transform *individual* participation into *personal* participation, and *collective* experience into a *communal* experience. Put differently, in a dialectic of increasing openness and deepening response, the mutual effort to attain clarity and stronger contact with truth and reality can elevate *discussion* to a true interpersonal *dialogue* of learning.

Discussion which emphasizes conformity to predetermined views or the correctness of individual response, which is couched in "denatured" language, or which emphasizes answers more than questions will clearly circumscribe the depth and quality of personal experience. In order for participation to be *personal*, it will be based not simply on abstract ideas, but on the experience of formulating an explicit idea of one's own; not simply on knowledge, but on the personal experience of knowing; not simply on speaking, but on words which strive to express their interior origin; not simply on words, but on the "space" of silence in which we can become better attuned to the experience in which our authentic words are formed; not simply on listening, but on openness and attentiveness; not simply on responding, but on opening to a deeper response; and not simply on an integrated experience of self, but relatedly, on the common and unifying experience of trying to better know and communicate the truth. Dialogue, in accordance with the person-centered principles of nonviolence, will aim to clarify and deepen perspective, and to communicate directly, personally, and as much as possible factually, at the same time endeavoring to strengthen the experience of common identity and relationship as persons. Whether involving literature, social studies, religion, philosophy, or other areas in which discussion will play a prominent role, it will be the effort to elevate discussion to dialogue that will most reflect a personalistic approach to teaching.

In a rare reflection on his own experience as a teacher, Merton wrote (in his journal, May, 1962): "I usually ignore this element in my own vocation, but obviously I am a writer, a student and a teacher as well as a contemplative of sorts, and my solitude etc., is that of a writer and teacher, not of a pure hermit. And the great thing in my life is, or should be, love of truth. I know there is nothing more precious than the bond of charity created by communicating and sharing the truth. This is really my whole life."[58] This might well be considered Merton's credo of teaching. In emphasizing the experience of relationship and love ("bond of charity") "created by communicating and sharing the truth," Merton testifies to his fundamental belief in the accessibility and transforming power of truth for each person and for the community of persons gathered in an effort to share and learn. The effort to discern, communicate, and share the truth intrinsic to dialogue, therefore, can renew and form the whole person in the experience of love and relationship made possible by this effort. This fundamental quality of experience will be vital to the formation of the whole person.

In addition to interpersonal dialogue, there is another realm of dialogue which can be offered as important to the formation of the whole person; Merton's interpretation of an idea of St. Augustine's that he introduces in *The New Man* suggests it.

St. Augustine, according to Merton, in contrast to those whose sense of the value of work is oriented to money or ambition or "cupidity," perceives work as a "dialogue with reality, and therefore as a conversation with God."[59] Particularly as it involves natural reality, work is by nature interactive, a matter of questioning and discovery and response, of giving and receiving, of balance and coordination. According to Merton, St. Augustine asks: "'Where can human reason better enter into a dialogue with the nature of things than when seeds have been planted, shoots laid out, shrubs transplanted, grafts inserted. It is as though one were questioning each root and seed, asking it what it can do and what it cannot do.'"[60] One can readily expand Augustine's humble and reverent perception of work to encompass dimensions of teaching and learning. Whether involving areas such as the natural sciences or the humanities, how might the effort at learning be enhanced if approached as a "dialogue with reality"?

Applied to the study of the physical and/or biological world, the metaphor of dialogue suggests, on the one hand, a process of questioning dedicated to asking and finding out about each thing, about its unique characteristics, about how it works and what it does (a more experimental knowledge[61]). Consistent with the formation of the faculties of seeing and hearing, it suggests knowledge and understanding which will strengthen concrete relationship, if not existential identification, with reality. Merton himself saw the possibility for this sort of experience in the most highly developed areas of science.[62] After a brief but wholehearted attempt at reading about current work in quantum physics one morning during breakfast at the hermitage, for example, he enthused: "Neils Bohr and Co. are definitely among my number one culture heroes. This magnificent instrument of thought they developed to understand what is happening in matter, what energy really is about—with their confrontation of the kind of thing Herakleitos [a Greek philosopher of the 5th century B.C.] was reaching for by intuition. It is terribly exciting, though I can't grasp any of it due to the fact that I have never had even high school physics and the equations are just hieroglyphics that represent to me no known animal."[63]

Whether practiced in the framework of interpersonal discussion or the study of the natural world, dialogue will be oriented to opening and clarifying perspective, to creating a full opportunity to discern, communicate, and share the truth, to establishing a greater contact with reality, and to enabling one to relate and respond to the world more freely and wholly. This was certainly Merton's orientation as a teacher, and, as several of his classes and former students indicate, was in many ways reflected in his own "manner of approach."

Like Mark Van Doren, Merton's interest in the development of intellectual integrity, in opening perspective, in fostering attentiveness, and in distinguishing the false from the real and true was reflected as much in his "manner of approach" as in the substance of his teaching. For example, in a conference addressing the question of the possible role of liberal arts in the education of a monk (January 14, 1962), Merton introduces the topic in a way designed to evoke his students' personal intellectual response. His approach is typically unassuming and natural, yet direct and sincere: "To sort of get down to this confusion, and to sort of handle it, I'll start out with just a plain, simple sentence . . . and then we'll try to take the thing apart a little bit: MONKS SHOULD RENOUNCE ALL LITERATURE. Now what about that? I [don't] want to ask for an official answer; what I want to know is: are you thinking?"[64] Merton's unpretentious manner, and his emphasis on "thinking," on formulating a personal rather than an "official" response, corresponds notably with his description of Mark Van Doren's teaching. It suggests as well his effort to establish an openness beyond "official" or preconceived notions, so that from "confusion" a clearer perspective might be established. Even in this very focused context, Merton was interested in engaging his students in the effort to distinguish insofar as possible the false from the true.

Just as in his writing Merton often states what something (such as the "self") is not in order to more clearly establish what it is, he typically in his teaching tried to identify and dispel illusion as part of the effort to discern the true and real. Merton's conference on "mass communication" is illustrative. Merton begins by asking a series of questions focused on the essential issues of his topic: "How do you get informed about what the world is? How do you get informed when you're in the world? Do you get informed? . . . Do mass communications really inform? If they don't what do they do? What should you get?"[65] He then illustrates the superficial treatment of such crucial issues as the race problem and poverty by the mass media. After pointing out these examples of impersonal reporting, Merton offers the alternative perspective of Thich Nhat Hanh's compelling, personal account of the war in Vietnam.[66] Again, it is the "person-oriented" approach (not only in the sense that the focus is on individual persons, but also because it reflects compassionate consideration of the whole person) which is most authentic for Merton.

Merton's personalism is especially evident in a class on St. Bernard that he conducted for novice monks at Gethsemani monastery in the early 1960s. Carefully, gently, with no apparent concern for time, he sets the stage for actual consideration of St. Bernard's work ("It's like the first time you eat Chinese food . . . it takes a long preparation to really get used to what he's trying to do."). He notes that he will not give "a big course on St. Bernard"—"that would be just like school again, there would be no point in doing that." Rather, he says, "What I can do, and what I really intend to do, is not to talk about St. Bernard exclusively, but to talk about *us*." Merton is not concerned so much with his students' understanding of the intellectual import of St. Bernard's writing as with their appreciation of the *experience*, the "resonances" or "echoes," which his words imply. In becoming attuned to the "resonances" of experience which St. Bernard's words evoke, Merton hopes that his students will be better able, along with him, to "transpose" them "into our time and our way of looking at things." Merton aims to open his students to a form of experiential communication and to encourage their own personal, experiential response. He orients his pedagogy accordingly: "I'm gonna get off to a real slow start on St. Bernard, exceedingly slow, so slow we'll cover about 10 lines . . . so slow and so detailed, probably most of you will be in despair! . . . You just be patient and I'll struggle with this thing."[67]

Merton's teaching, like Mark Van Doren's, can be described as "sapiential." In addition to naturally drawing on the Christian spiritual and biblical tradition that he shared with his fellow monks, Merton expanded discussion of basic aspects of human (especially spiritual) experience with comparative and illustrative reference to stories from the Hasidic and Sufi traditions in the Gethsemani conferences during the 1960s.[68] He also introduced the sapiential through his teaching of literature (in both his writing and his conferences), as mentioned above, addressing in particular the work of such writers as William Blake, Rainer Maria Rilke, William Faulkner, and Albert Camus.[69] Beyond spiritual theology and literature, Merton spoke to the sapiential through such topics as the "cargo movements" of the South Pacific (derived from the anthropological study that helped him in writing *The Geography of Lograire*) and Reza Arasteh's work on "final integration in the adult personality."[70] Merton's "free interpretive readings" of Chuang Tzu, the Chinese philosopher of the fourth and third centuries, B.C. (presented in *The Way of Chuang Tzu*), also indicate his effort to introduce others to parables, fables, or "funny" stories which might act as a bridge to a more "direct existential grasp of reality."[71] Merton's collection of the stories and sayings of the "Desert Fathers," Christian hermits of the fourth century, had a like purpose (they enable us "to reopen the sources that have been polluted or blocked up . . . they flow from an experience of the deeper levels of life."[72]). Merton's encouragement of a monastic education that was sapientially as well as theologically oriented was to some extent exemplified in his own teaching; indeed, in the example of his ongoing self-education.[73]

One of Merton's distinguished students at Gethsemani, Fr. John Eudes Bamberger (at one time Merton's personal physician, later abbot of the Trappist Abbey of the Genesee), recalls that Merton "was both down-to-earth in his expression and yet often brilliant and concerned for the highest realities in his focus."[74] Brother Patrick Hart, also a former student as well as personal secretary to Merton, remarks that "Merton was one of the very great teachers that I have had the good fortune to meet in my life. . . . [He] had the ability to bring out the best in his students."[75] In Brother Patrick's remarks one hears an echo of those qualities that Merton valued in his own teaching mentors.

Together, the observations of Fr. Bamberger and Brother Patrick capture a vital dimension of both Merton's teaching and his learning—the unassuming, yet total effort to open himself and others to more concrete, experiential, personal contact with reality and truth, with people and life, with the hidden wholeness and presence of God.[76] This effort recalls Merton's declaration, in his essay "Learning to Live," that "the purpose of all learning is to dispose [one] for [self-discovery]."[77] It likewise brings to mind Merton's messages to Japanese readers of *The Seven Storey Mountain*: "These pages invite [the reader] to listen for [him or her] self"; and "I seek to speak to you, in some way, as your own self."[78]

Merton spoke to what was essential and to the whole, inviolate person. His was a "living pedagogy"; his approach and his aim were united by love of person and truth; as he lived and learned and loved, so did he teach.

Of the scholar Ananda K. Coomaraswamy, Merton once wrote, "[He] was a voice bearing witness to the truth, and he wanted nothing but for others to receive that truth in their own way, in agreement with their own mental and spiritual context. As if there was any other way of accepting it."[79] These words might very well be applied to Merton himself and more broadly to teaching which would bear on the formation of the whole person.

Teaching which would serve the formation of the whole person will clearly be guided by these broad questions: To what extent is the approach "person-oriented"? Does it exemplify seeing, hearing, speaking, communicating, and dialoguing as areas in which the growth of the whole person can to some degree be realized? To what extent does it involve the *whole* person, and the community of persons, in "communicating and sharing the truth?"

A truly person-oriented approach to teaching will attend to the interior freedom and experience of the person; to, more specifically, interior openness, attentiveness and response; to sincere, personal expression; to the personal capacity to apprehend and relate to reality and truth. Provision for questioning and silence and the opportunity to engage in genuine dialogue with others and with reality will characterize the effort to teach and learn.

Notes

1. Merton to Mary Declan Martin, April 4, 1968 (Louisville, Ky., Bellarmine College, Thomas Merton Studies Center).

2. Merton, "On Remembering M. Delmas," in Morris Ernst, ed., *The Teacher* (Englewood Cliffs, N. J.: Prentice-Hall, 1967), pp. 47-53.

3. Merton, *The Seven Storey Mountain*, pp. 139-141.

4. Ibid., p. 139.

5. Ibid., p. 180; see also Merton's essays in Hart, ed., *The Literary Essays of Thomas Merton*.

6. Ibid., p. 140.

7. Ibid., p. 139.

8. I would suggest, among others, Eleanor Duckworth's piece on "The Having of Wonderful Ideas," *Harvard Educational Review* 51:1; pp. 217-231, to illustrate teaching that allows for this quality of conception rather than reception of knowledge.

9. Merton, "Christianity and Totalitarianism," in *Disputed Questions*, p. 148; I introduce this thought in Chapter 3; see also Merton's essay, "A Devout Meditation in Memory of Adolph Eichmann," in *Raids*.

10. Merton, *The Seven Storey Mountain*, p. 139.

11. Ibid., p. 140.

12. Conference Tape 306B, "Monastic Education," September 17, 1968 (Louisville, Ky., Bellarmine College: Thomas Merton Studies Center, unpublished tape).

13. Merton, "'Baptism in the Forest,'" in Hart, ed., *Literary Essays*.

14. Ibid., p. 99. (See also discussion in Chapter 6.)

15. Ibid., p. 100.

16. Ibid., p. 98.

17. Merton, "Learning to Live," in *Love and Living*, p. 9.

18. Merton, "The Need for a New Education," in *Contemplation in a World of Action*, p. 202.

19. Merton, *The Seven Storey Mountain*, p. 219.

20. Merton, "On Remembering M. Delmas," in Ernst, ed., *The Teacher*, p. 50.

21. Ibid., p. 52.

22. Ibid.

23. Ibid., p. 51.

24. Ibid., p. 52.

25. Ibid.

26. Merton to James Forest, February 21, 1966, in Shannon, ed., *The Hidden Ground of Love*, pp. 294-297. (See also Chapter 5.)

27. Parker Palmer, *To Know As We Are Known: A Spirituality of Education* (New York: Harper & Row, 1983).

28. Ibid., p. 81.

29. Ibid.

30. Thomas Merton, "Psychology of Attention," Notes in *Collected Essays*, vol. 16 (unpublished, Gethsemani Abbey, Trappist, Kentucky), p. 37.

31. Ibid.

32. Merton to Abdul Aziz, January 2, 1966, in Shannon, ed., *The Hidden Ground of Love*, p. 63.

33. See Michael Mott's comments, *The Seven Mountains of Thomas Merton*, p. 601. (Refer to note #32.)

34. Matthew Kelty, "The Man," in Hart, ed., *Thomas Merton/Monk*, p. 20.

35. See, for example, Mott, *The Seven Mountains of Thomas Merton*, p. 373; In a passage from Merton's personal journal (restricted from publication until 1993) that Mott records, Merton laments submitting the draft of an article prematurely: "Better to have waited and simply tried to say, with utmost care, what is true. Of course, when I write anything I write what I think is true. But what is true can also be said so badly that it becomes a misrepresentation of the truth."

36. Merton to Abdul Aziz, January 16, 1968, in Shannon, ed., *The Hidden Ground of Love*, p. 66.

37. By extension, this approach can apply equally well to reading, writing, and listening in general—not simply as academic disciplines, but as disciplines through which one tries to better grasp or express a particular knowledge, or truth, Cf., Simone Weil, "Reflections on the Right Use of School Studies," in *Waiting for God*.

38. See Merton to Abdul Aziz, January 2, 1966, in Shannon, ed., *The Hidden Ground of Love*, p. 63. "Strictly speaking," Merton writes, "I have a very simple way of prayer. It is centered entirely on attention to the presence of God and to His Will and His Love."

39. Simone Weil, "Attention and Will," in Siân Miles, ed., *Simone Weil: An Anthology* (New York: Weidenfeld and Nicolson, 1986), p. 214.

40. Ibid., p. 212.

41. Merton to Wilbur H. Ferry, December 12, 1967, in Shannon, ed., *The Hidden Ground of Love*, p. 236.

42. The depth and breadth of Merton's "literary" correspondence can hardly be captured here; like his correspondence with religious leaders and scholars such as D. T. Suzuki, Abdul Aziz, and Abraham Heschel, it signifies another area in which Merton's intellectual openness and creativity were fostered through personal correspondence.

43. Merton to Laura Knight, March 23, 1968 (Louisville, Ky., Bellarmine College: Thomas Merton Studies Center). Merton also writes to Knight, a high-school junior at the time: "I like the monastic life, I like to meditate and be alone with God. But I also think a lot about the troubles of the world . . . for you can't claim to love God if you are not interested in people. I try to help people by my writing. Sometimes they get a little mad at the things I say, but I don't care: I want to express the truth as I see it."

44. Merton to Nancy Fly Bredenberg, November 28, 1967 (Louisville, Ky., Bellarmine College: Thomas Merton Studies Center).

45. Merton to Nancy Fly Bredenberg, April, 22, 1968.

46. Merton to Suzanne Butorovich, June 22, 1967 (Louisville, Ky., Bellarmine College: Thomas Merton Studies Center).

47. Merton to Suzanne Butorovich, July 18, 1967.

48. Merton to Suzanne Butorovich, October 7, 1967.

49. Merton to Suzanne Butorovich, July 18, 1967.

50. Ibid.

51. Merton to Suzanne Butorovich, June 4, 1968.

52. Michael Mott provides a comprehensive and illustrative example of the fruitfulness of Merton's correspondence with Czeslaw Milosz; see Mott, *The Seven Mountains of Thomas Merton*, pp. 354-359.

53. Merton to Wilbur H. Ferry, March 6, 1962, in Shannon, ed., *The Hidden Ground of Love*, p. 209.

54. Mott, *The Seven Mountains of Thomas Merton*, pp. 354-359.

55. See Merton, *Zen and the Birds of Appetite*, pp. 99-141.

56. These conferences were taped and are available for listening review at the Thomas Merton Studies Center; Merton, "Nhat Hanh Is My Brother," in *The Nonviolent Alternative*, pp. 263-264.

57. Merton to John Heidbrink, November 26, 1964, in Shannon, ed., *The Hidden Ground of Love*, p. 417. See Chapter 5 for discussion of this conference.

58. Recorded by Mott from Merton's restricted journals; Mott, *The Seven Mountains of Thomas Merton*, p. 641 (note 75).

59. Merton, *The New Man*, p. 81.

60. Ibid.

61. Ibid.

62. See, for example, Merton, "The Need for a New Education," in *Contemplation in a World of Action*, p. 203.

63. Quoted from Merton's restricted journals by John Howard Griffin, *Follow the Ecstasy*, p. 157.

64. Conference Tape #43, "Liberal Arts—Good or Bad?" January 14, 1962 (Louisville, Ky., Bellarmine College: Thomas Merton Studies Center, unpublished tape). One need not listen long to the tapes of Merton's conferences to appreciate his sincerity and unpretentiousness, as well as his sense of humor.

65. Conference Tape #242, "Mass Communication," May 22, 1962.

66. See Chapter 6 (section on "Communication") for elaboration.

67. Merton Tape, "Love Casts Out Fear," Side A (Kansas City, Mo.: Credence Cassettes, 1988).

68. Listen, for example, to Conference Tape #265B, "Growing up Beyond Social World," February 18, 1968, or Tape #4B, "Solitude, Community, and Poverty," *Mystic Life Series* (Chappaqua, N.Y.: Electronic Paperbacks, 1976).

69. For example, Merton's discussion of the poet Rainer Maria Rilke, recorded on "Love and the Search for God" (Kansas City, Mo.: Credence Cassettes, 1988); see also Brother Patrick Hart's remarks in his introduction to *The Literary Essays of Thomas Merton*, pp. xiv, xv.

70. Conference Tapes #295, "Cargo," and 265B "Growing Up Beyond Social World" (Thomas Merton Studies Center, Bellarmine College).

71. Merton, *The Way of Chuang Tzu*, p. 11.

72. Merton, *The Wisdom of the Desert* (New York: New Directions, 1960), p. 11.

73. See Merton, "The Need for a New Education," in *Contemplation in a World of Action*.

74. Father John Eudes Bamberger to the author, October 20, 1986.

75. Brother Patrick Hart to the author, July 30, 1986.

76. See Matthew Kelty's essay, "The Man," in Hart, ed., *Thomas Merton/Monk*, pp. 19-35, for a more detailed description of Merton's personal qualities, particularly his simplicity and genuineness.

77. Merton, "Learning to Live," in *Love and Living*, p. 9.

78. Daggy, ed., *Introductions*, p. 47.

79. Merton to Dona Luisa Coomaraswamy, February 12, 1961, in Shannon, ed., *The Hidden Ground of Love*, p. 129.

8

Summary

Merton's thoughts on education, as they are explicitly recorded, are provocative, but brief and general. He summarized in a
letter that education "means the formation of the whole person"
(Chapter 2); he designated its purpose as "self-discovery," a
major theme in his essay "Learning To Live" (Chapter 3). In a
discussion on monastic education, he notes that "education
should be something broad and deep . . . a consistent broadening and deepening process to give us not only knowledge but
also wisdom; it should be an opening up and developing of the
human capacities of each one of us" (Chapter 7). Reflecting on
his own teaching, Merton suggested also that education involves
learning to communicate and share the truth (Chapter 7). As
pithy as these references to education are, they become magnified enormously in scope and depth when set against the rich
background of Merton's life, his spiritual and social writing, his
creative expression, and his Christian contemplative perspectives nurtured in the midst of the twentieth century.

Merton's ideas regarding education cannot be fully understood outside the context of his Christian faith and contemplative experience, yet neither can they be fully appreciated without recognizing them as his deepest understanding of, and
hopes for, human growth and experience in general. Merton's
understanding of the whole person is rooted in his theological
belief and spiritual faith in the unified transcendent and indwelling presence of Christ, in Christ identified with each person. Yet, at the same time, he explains in the more universal

terms of concrete human experience that we can only know the whole person through love and compassion; as he wrote to Dorothy Day, "Persons are known . . . only by love."[1] The difference between what Merton expresses theologically on the basis of faith and what he expresses in terms of concrete human experience can be explained, at least conceptually (for Merton they are interrelated), as the difference between a strictly religious and what he came to describe as a "sapiential" outlook. The sapiential perspective, as Merton explains in one of his literary essays, "embraces the entire scope of [the person's] life in all its meaning."[2] It was this quality of wisdom, an existential grasp of life at its very roots, which his Christian contemplative perspective helped him to deeply appreciate, and which drew forth his admiration of the work of writers such as William Faulkner and teachers such as Mark Van Doren. He could not overstate the importance of a sapiential sensibility for his society, particularly given the challenges posed to a fundamental sense of human meaning and identity by the complex social, technological, political, and ideological changes affecting the people of his day. Both Merton's religious and "sapiential" perspectives are essential to understanding what education whose purpose is "self-discovery" and which involves "the formation of the whole person" means.

"Self-discovery" refers to the experience, at the inmost ground of our contingent being, of our true, existential identity in God, the ground of all being. The "whole person" can be described as the subject of that inviolate identity, the person free to live and love in the fullness of being. Education which involves "the formation of the whole person" will in some way exemplify this understanding of the whole person as an integral part of the effort at formation; in other words, the quality of such education will be fully personal. "Formation" is thus not interpreted here to suggest an objectified set of means and ends but rather a quality of increasing openness and increasingly deeper and more integrated response in an experiential level of wholeness. Since it involves the whole person, this level hardly excludes, but ultimately subsumes, reason and analysis. This implies a quality of "knowledge" beyond facts, concepts, and intuition, a "knowing" with one's whole self, possible because of the subjective and contingent quality of being (what Merton suggests is sapiential knowledge).[3]

The ideas of "self-discovery" and "the formation of the whole person," when viewed in light of Merton's life and work, implicate several fundamental areas of personal growth which can be fostered by education. These include especially "seeing," "hearing," "speaking," "voice," and a corresponding quality of communication and dialogue.

"Seeing" and "hearing" (Chapter 4) are sensory metaphors which indicate our capacity, as persons, to apprehend the unique and concrete identity of natural things and, moreover, the "hidden wholeness" of Being which each uniquely intimates. Hence, they indicate the faculties by which we become more open to our intimate relationship with reality. When we see and hear things more as they are (recognizing first their "value and beauty"), and more as a sign of a deeper reality in which with them we are also identified, then we are better able to use and live with them more respectfully, if not, as Merton writes, "in and for God."[4] And our ability to enter into a fruitful "dialogue with reality" (Chapter 7) is likewise enhanced.

"Speaking" (Chapter 4) is not simply the capacity to say what we want to say but rather what we truly understand and mean as reflected in our deepest experience. The authenticity of our speech will be in proportion to our openness and attentiveness to the origin of our words in the silence and freedom of our own inner experience. Like seeing and hearing, the development of the capacity for speech, implying both oral and written expression, will be integral to the formation of the whole person.

The ability to form words representing our authentic relation to a situation will be vital to the development of our personal "voice"—our capacity to speak compassionately and honestly in fidelity to life, person, and truth (Chapter 5). When we begin to exercise our ability to speak in open and honest response to truth, then we will grow in our ability to communicate sincerely, creatively, freely, and authentically, and to participate more fully in dialogue and community life (Chapter 6).

Insofar as it emerges from authentic voice, communication, too, will be authentic; it will be a sincere expression of our deepest personal experience. Correspondingly, our approach to dialogue will be focused by a recognition of the other as person. Our effort will be directed to establishing, in humility and trust, the mutual openness in which we will be more "awake," better able to see, hear, and respond more wholly to truth, and better able to relate more trustingly and lovingly to each other.

Of vital importance to our growth as whole persons will be our service to others and our sense of vocation. Though little more than alluded to (Chapter 3), these dimensions of the formation of the whole person deserve mention here. In proportion as we give to others, in love and through our particular vocations, we will, as Merton so often says, become more real; we will realize ourselves more as whole persons. Through "charity" (as with art and worship), Merton suggests that we can in fact discover "a new and transcendent meaning" in "the midst of ordinary life."[5] These dimensions of our growth as whole persons must certainly be considered well within the realm of education as Merton understood it.

Growth in the areas of seeing and hearing, speaking and personal voice, communication and dialogue is not growth in a linear sense but more a deeper realization of who we *are*; that is, of our capacity to *be*. Our formation as whole persons cannot be measured simply in terms of what we can do, or what we know; we are not what is outside ourselves, or as Merton put it in his Japanese introduction to *The Seven Storey Mountain*, "object[s] of interest."[6] Ultimately, our "doing" will emerge freely from our "being," essentially, from love.

Education which involves "the formation of the whole person" has a definite analogy in teaching (Chapter 7). Teaching which in some way embodies this understanding of what education means will be "person-oriented."

While certainly not precluded, person-oriented teaching will not attend simply to the individual acquisition of particular skills and knowledge; nor will it focus on the achievement of measurable visible results as an index of personal growth. In keeping with Merton's understanding of the person, it will be concerned ultimately with intrinsic experience rather than extrinsic information.

Not as a technique, but as a humble, living and loving expression of regard for the other as person, person-oriented teaching will attend to the capacities for personal growth intrinsic to the person and, more fundamentally, to that quality of interior experience which grounds our capacities to see and hear attuned to reality, and to speak and communicate in conformity with truth. This will entail, in part, dialogue which "educes" personal ideas, which provides "space" for each person to attend silently to the origin and formation of words expressive of personal experience, and which cultivates mutual openness and responsiveness to truth; also, in part, engaging in a "dialogue with reality," implying, particularly in the area of science, not only broader understanding of the essential qualities and identity of things, but a deeper awareness and enrichment of our relationship to reality. In such dialogue we participate in (not dominate) a living relationship with others and reality ("communion") as an aspect of our own being and wholeness. When teaching is based thus on respect for the inviolate whole person, and creates the opportunity for "communicating and sharing the truth," then education involving "the formation of the whole person" will be realized as a living pedagogy.

Merton's ideas on education do not originate in an ideology or philosophy but rather in an experience of reality and being informed by his Christian faith; more specifically, by faith in the living reality of Christ. They are thus deeply grounded, suggesting an approach to education from a profound existential perspective.

Merton's ideas are not a response to the self-reflective questions "Who am I?" or "What can I do?" but rather a response to the living existential reality, "I am," and, moreover, "I am with others." This response is very much shaped by and rooted in human experience. It is this fundamental groundedness which distinguishes Merton's ideas and their implications and suggests their significance in an age that so often judges meaning and relationship on the basis of external criteria and evidence.

Amid the ineluctable flow of change that affects the material conditions of our lives, and which implicitly or explicitly questions our most basic perspectives on what it means to live as persons, we will need to evaluate our efforts at education on a fully human scale, and consider whether, in fact, they enable us, as Merton would say, to be more who we already are. We might then look to Merton's living example, more than to his ideas, to his effort to be authentically no more or less than who he was, and then seek to discover that capacity in ourselves.

Notes

1. Merton to Dorothy Day, December 20, 1961, in Shannon, ed., *The Hidden Ground of Love*, p. 141.

2. Merton, "'Baptism in the Forest'," in Hart, ed., *The Literary Essays of Thomas Merton*, p. 99.

3. Ibid., pp. 100-102, passim.

4. Merton, *New Seeds*, p. 21.

5. Merton, "Poetry and Contemplation: A Reappraisal," in Hart, ed., *The Literary Essays of Thomas Merton*, pp. 340-341.

6. Daggy, ed., *Introductions*, p. 45.

Bibliography

Andersen, Hans Christian. *Eighty Fairy Tales.* New York: Pantheon Books, 1976.

Buber, Martin. *I and Thou.* New York: Charles Scribner's Sons, 1970.

Daggy, Robert, editor. *Introductions East and West: The Foreign Prefaces of Thomas Merton.* Greensboro, North Carolina: Unicorn Press, 1981.

Dillard, Annie. *Pilgrim at Tinker Creek.* New York: Bantam Books, 1974.

Duckworth, Eleanor. "The Having of Wonderful Ideas," *Harvard Education Review,* 51 (1), 1972, 217-231.

Ernst, Morris, editor. *The Teacher.* Englewood Cliffs, N.J.: Prentice-Hall, Inc., 1967.

Griffin, John Howard. *Follow the Ecstasy.* Fort Worth, Tx.: Latitudes Press, 1983.

Hart, Brother Patrick, editor. *The Legacy of Thomas Merton.* Kalamazoo, Mich.: Cistercian Publications, 1986.

Hart, Brother Patrick, editor. *The Literary Essays of Thomas Merton.* New York: New Directions, 1981.

Hart, Brother Patrick, editor. *The Message of Thomas Merton.* Kalamazoo, Mich.: Cistercian Publications, 1981.

Hart, Brother Patrick, editor. *Thomas Merton / Monk: A Monastic Tribute.* Kalamazoo, Mich.: Cistercian Publications, 1983.

Heschel, Abraham. *A Passion for Truth.* New York: Farrar, Straus & Giroux, 1973.

Johnston, William, editor. *The Cloud of Unknowing.* Garden City, N.Y.: Image Books, 1973.

King, Martin Luther, Jr. *Stride Toward Freedom.* San Francisco, Cal.: Harper & Row, Publishers, 1958.

McDonnell, Thomas P., editor. *A Thomas Merton Reader.* Rev. Ed. Garden City, N.Y.: Image Books, 1974.

Merton, Thomas. *The Asian Journal of Thomas Merton.* New York: New Directions, 1975.

Merton, Thomas. *The Behavior of Titans.* New York: New Directions, 1961.

Merton, Thomas. *Clement of Alexandria: Selections From the Protreptikos.* New York: New Directions, 1962.

Merton, Thomas. "Cold War Letters." Unpublished, 1961-62. Louisville, Kentucky, Bellarmine College: Thomas Merton Studies Center.

Merton, Thomas. *The Collected Essays of Thomas Merton.* Unpublished bound collection. Trappist, Kentucky: Gethsemani Abbey.

Merton, Thomas. *Conjectures of a Guilty Bystander.* Garden City, N.Y.: Image Books, 1965.

Merton, Thomas. *Contemplation in a World of Action.* Garden City, N.Y.: Doubleday and Company, Inc., 1971.

Merton, Thomas. *The Day of a Stranger.* Edited by Robert E. Daggy. Salt Lake City, Utah: Gibbs M. Smith, Inc., 1981.

Merton, Thomas. *Disputed Questions.* New York: Harcourt Brace Jovanovich, 1960.

Merton, Thomas. *Faith and Violence.* Notre Dame, Ind.: University of Notre Dame Press, 1968.

Merton, Thomas, editor. *Gandhi on Nonviolence.* New York: New Directions, 1965.

Merton, Thomas. *The Geography of Lograire.* New York: New Directions, 1969.

Merton, Thomas. *Hagia Sophia.* Lexington, Ky.: Stamperia del Santuccio, 1962.

Merton, Thomas. "The Inner Experience: Notes on Contemplation (I)," *Cistercian Studies,* XVIII (1), 1983, 3-15.

Merton, Thomas. "The Inner Experience: Society and the Inner Self (II)," *Cistercian Studies,* XVIII (2), 1983, 121-134.

Merton, Thomas. "The Inner Experience: Christian Contemplation (III)," *Cistercian Studies,* XVIII (3), 1983, 201-216.

Merton, Thomas. "The Inner Experience: Problems of the Contemplative Life (VII)," *Cistercian Studies,* XIX (3), 1984, 267-282.

Merton, Thomas. "The Inner Experience: Prospects and Conclusions (VIII)," *Cistercian Studies,* XIX (4), 1984, 336-345.

Merton, Thomas. *Ishi Means Man: Essays on Native Americans.* Greensboro, N.C.: Unicorn Press, 1976.

Merton, Thomas. *Life and Holiness.* New York: Image Books, 1963.

Merton, Thomas. *Love and Living.* Edited by Naomi Burton Stone and Brother Patrick Hart. New York: Bantam Books, 1979.

Merton, Thomas. *The Monastic Journey.* Edited by Brother Patrick Hart. Mission, Kan.: Sheed Andrews and McMeel, Inc., 1977.

Merton, Thomas. *Mystics and Zen Masters.* New York: Farrar, Straus & Giroux, 1967.

Merton, Thomas. *The New Man.* New York: Farrar, Straus & Giroux, 1961.

Merton, Thomas. *New Seeds of Contemplation.* New York: New Directions, 1961.

Merton, Thomas. *No Man Is an Island.* New York: Harcourt Brace Jovanovich, 1955.

Merton, Thomas. *The Nonviolent Alternative.* Edited by Gordon Zahn. New York: Farrar, Straus & Giroux, 1980.

Merton, Thomas. *Opening the Bible.* Collegeville, Minn.: The Liturgical Press, 1970.

Merton, Thomas. "THE POORER MEANS: A Meditation on Ways to Unity," *Sobernost,* 5:2 (Winter-Spring, 1966), 74-79.

Merton, Thomas. *Raids on the Unspeakable.* New York: New Directions, 1966.

Merton, Thomas. *Seasons of Celebration.* New York: Farrar, Straus & Giroux, 1965.

Merton, Thomas. *The Secular Journal of Thomas Merton.* New York: Farrar, Straus & Giroux, 1959.

Merton, Thomas. *Seeds of Destruction.* New York: Farrar, Straus & Giroux, 1964.

Merton, Thomas. *Selected Poems of Thomas Merton.* (enlarged edition). New York: New Directions, 1967.

Merton, Thomas. *The Seven Storey Mountain.* New York: Harcourt Brace Jovanovich, Inc., 1948.

Merton, Thomas. *The Sign of Jonas.* Garden City, N.Y.: Image Books, 1953.

Merton, Thomas. *Spiritual Direction and Meditation.* Collegeville, Minn.: The Liturgical Press, 1960.

Merton, Thomas. *Thoughts in Solitude.* New York: Farrar, Straus & Giroux, 1958.

Merton, Thomas. *A Vow of Conversation.* Edited by Naomi Burton Stone. New York: Farrar, Straus & Giroux, 1988.

Merton, Thomas. *The Way of Chuang Tzu.* New York: New Directions, 1965.

Merton, Thomas. *What is Contemplation?* Springfield, Ill.: Templegate Publishers, 1978.

Merton, Thomas. *The Wisdom of the Desert.* New York: New Directions, 1960.

Merton, Thomas. *Zen and the Birds of Appetite.* New York: New Directions, 1968.

Miles, Siân, editor. *Simone Weil: An Anthology.* New York: Weidenfeld and Nicolson, 1986.

Mott, Michael. *The Seven Mountains of Thomas Merton.* Boston, Mass.: Houghton Mifflin Company, 1984.

Nhat Hanh, Thich. *The Miracle of Mindfulness.* Boston, Mass.: Beacon Press, 1975.

Nouwen, Henri J. M. *The Genesee Diary: Report from a Trappist Monastery.* Garden City, N.Y.: Image Books, 1976.

Nouwen, Henri J. M. "Introduction to Spirituality." Course Handouts. Cambridge, Mass.: Harvard Divinity School, 1984.

Nouwen, Henri J. M. *Thomas Merton: Contemplative Critic.* San Francisco, Cal.: Harper & Row, Publishers, 1972.

Palmer, Parker. *To Know As We Are Known / A Spirituality of Education.* San Francisco, Cal.: Harper & Row, Publishers, 1983.

Pasternak, Boris. *Dr. Zhivago.* New York: Signet Books, 1958.

Patnaik, Deba Prasad. *Geography of Holiness: The Photography of Thomas Merton.* New York: The Pilgrim Press, 1980.

Shannon, William, editor. *The Hidden Ground of Love: The Letters of Thomas Merton on Religious Experience and Social Concerns.* New York: Farrar, Straus & Giroux, 1985.

Thoreau, Henry David. *Walden and Other Writings.* New York: Bantam Books, Inc., 1962.

Weil, Simone. *Waiting for God.* New York: G. P. Putnam's Sons, 1951.

Woodcock, George. *Thomas Merton, Monk and Poet: A Critical Study.* Edinburgh: Canongate Publishing, Ltd., 1978.

MERTON CONFERENCE TAPES
(Thomas Merton Studies Center, Bellarmine College, Louisville, Kentucky)

Conference Tape #32 ("Christian Learning, St. Aug.")

Conference Tape #85A ("Love and False Self in St. Paul")

Conference Tape #119A ("Natural Experience of God"), August 25, 1963.

Conference Tape #135B ("Silence and Making Signs—Interior Word Behind Speech")

Conference Tape #242A ("Mass Communication"), May 22, 1966.

Conference Tape #242B ("Description of Vietnamese Monk's Visit"), May 29, 1966.

Conference Tape #265B ("Growing Up Beyond Social World"), February 2, 1968.

Conference Tape #289B ("Nonviolence, Authority, Progress")

Conference Tape #306A ("Easter Homily"), September 17, 1968.

Conference Tape #306B ("Monastic Education"), September 17, 1968.

CONFERENCE TAPES (COMMERCIAL)

Conference Tape (B) ("Solitude, Community and Poverty"), *Mystic Life Series* (4). Chappaqua, N.Y.: Electronic-Paperbacks, 1976.

Conference Tape (A&B) ("The Thirst for God," "The Spiritual Life of the Heart"), *Mystic Life Series* (7). Chappaqua, N.Y.: Electronic-Paperbacks, 1976.

"Beauty is from God." Kansas City, Missouri: Credence Cassettes, National Catholic Reporter Publishing Co. 1988.

"Love and the Search for God." Kansas City, Missouri: Credence Cassettes, National Catholic Reporter Publishing Co., 1988.

"Love Casts Out Fear." Kansas City, Missouri: Credence Cassettes, National Catholic Reporter Publishing Co., 1988.

CORRESPONDENCE FILES
(Thomas Merton Studies Center, Bellarmine College, Louisville, Kentucky)

Letters from and to Nancy Fly Bredenberg (11/28/67 - 4/22/68)

Letter to John B. Brown (8/7/68)

Letters from and to Suzanne Butorovich (6/15/67 - 6/4/68)

Letter to Philip J. Cascia (2/16/68)

Letter to Neil Cram (4/28/68)

Letter to George Lewis Fields (4/28/68)

Letter to Laura Knight (3/23/68)

Letters from and to Jacques Maritain (2/10/49 - 1/30/67)

Letter to Mary Declan Martin (4/26/68)

See Merton, Thomas. *The Road to Joy: Letters to New and Old Friends.* Edited by Robert E. Daggy. New York: Farrar, Straus & Giroux, 1989.

Index Of Names

Index Of Subjects

Advertising, 77, 133-34

"Atlas and the Fatman" (Merton), 98

Attention: described, 50, 73, 157-59; as educational discipline in formation of whole person, 10, 51, 55, 56, 57, 116, 157-61; Merton on, 72-73, 158; mentioned, 68; as mode of learning, 57, 157-61, 177; Simone Weil on, 50-51, 160-61; as spiritual discipline, 72-73, 157-58

Awakeness, 49-50, 160, 178

"'Baptism in the Forest': Wisdom and Initiation in William Faulkner" (Merton), 131

"Basis of Christian Nonviolence, The" (Merton), 146 (note 69)

"Blessed are the Meek: The Christian Roots of Nonviolence" (Merton), 47, 135, 136, 138

Cables to the Ace (Merton), 162

Catholic Peace Fellowship, 121 (note 68)

The Catholic Worker, 109, 121, (note 68)

Christian humanism: and Merton, 7-9

"Christianity and Totalitarianism" (Merton), 52, 150

The Cloud of Unknowing (anonymous), 60 (note 31)

"Cold War Letters" (Merton), 89, 90, 92, 94, 104, 106, 108, 125, 135

Communication: discussed, 54, 124-34, 142; and education, 134; experiential, 140-41, 168; and language, 132-34; and person-oriented thinking, 128-29; and propaganda, 125-26

Communion: as spiritual unity, 54, 140-43

Community: and Christ, 32; collectivity, contrast to, 47, 53; discussed, 51-54; and group discussion, 156, 164; personal basis for, 53-54; and self-discovery 32-33, 46-47, 55

Conferences (given by Merton): on "Authority, Progress," 106-107; on "Liberal Arts—Good